There's a Boy in the Girls' Bathroom

There's a Boy in the Girls' Bathroom

1판 1쇄 2013년 12월 9일
2판 2쇄 2024년 7월 1일

지은이 LOUIS SACHAR
기획 이수영
책임편집 차소향 김보경
콘텐츠제작및감수 차소향 김보경 Damon O
저작권 명채린
디자인 김진영
마케팅 두잉글 사업 본부

펴낸이 이수영
펴낸곳 롱테일북스
출판등록 제2015-000191호
주소 04033 서울특별시 마포구 양화로 113, 3층(서교동, 순흥빌딩)
전자메일 help@ltinc.net

ISBN 979-11-91343-96-0 14740

There's a Boy in the Girls' Bathroom

LOUIS SACHAR

WORKBOOK

Contents

'아동 도서계의 노벨상!' 미국 최고 권위의 아동 문학상

뉴베리 상(Newbery Award)은 미국 도서관 협회에서 해마다 미국 아동 문학 발전에 가장 크게 이바지한 작가에게 수여하는 아동 문학상입니다. 1922년에 시작된 이 상은 미국에서 가장 오랜 역사를 지닌 아동 문학상일 뿐 아니라, '아동 도서계의 노벨상'이라 불릴 만큼 최고의 권위를 자랑하고 있습니다.

뉴베리 상은 그 역사와 권위만큼이나 심사기준이 까다롭기로 유명한데, 심사단은 책의 주제의식은 물론 정보의 깊이와 스토리의 정교함, 캐릭터와 문체의 적정성 등을 꼼꼼히 평가하여 수상작을 결정합니다.

그해 최고의 작품으로 선정되면 금색 메달을 수여하기 때문에 '뉴베리 메달(Newbery Medal)'이라고 부르며, 후보에 올랐던 주목할 만한 작품들은 '뉴베리 아너(Newbery Honor)'라고 하여 은색 마크를 수여합니다.

뉴베리 상을 받게 되면 미국의 모든 도서관에 비치되어 더 많은 독자들을 만나게 되며, 대부분 수십에서 수백만 부가 판매되는 베스트셀러가 됩니다. 뿐만 아니라 뉴베리 상을 수상한 작가는 그만큼 필력과 작품성을 인정받게 되어, 수상작이 아닌 작품들도 수상작 못지않게 커다란 주목과 사랑을 받습니다.

왜 뉴베리 수상작인가?
쉬운 어휘로 쓰인 '검증된' 영어원서!

'뉴베리 수상작'들은 '검증된 원서'로 국내 영어 학습자들에게 큰 사랑을 받고 있습니다. '뉴베리 수상작'이 원서 읽기에 좋은 교재인 이유는 무엇일까요?

1. 아동 문학인 만큼 어휘가 어렵지 않습니다.
2. 어렵지 않은 어휘를 사용하면서도 '문학상'을 수상한 만큼 문장의 깊이가 상당합니다.
3. 적당한 난이도의 어휘와 깊이 있는 문장으로 구성되어 있기 때문에 초등 고학년부터 성인까지, 영어 초보자부터 실력자까지 모든 영어 학습자들이 읽기에 좋습니다.

실제로 뉴베리 수상작은 국제중·특목고에서는 입시 필독서로, 대학교에서는 영어 강독 교재로 다양하고 폭넓게 활용되고 있습니다. 이런 이유로 뉴베리 수상작은 한국어 번역서보다 오히려 원서가 훨씬 많이 판매되는 기현상을 보이고 있습니다.

'베스트 오브 베스트'만을 엄선한 「뉴베리 컬렉션」

「뉴베리 컬렉션」은 뉴베리 메달 및 아너 수상작, 그리고 뉴베리 수상 작가의 유명 작품들을 엄선하여 한국 영어 학습자들을 위한 최적의 교재로 재탄생시킨 영어 원서 시리즈입니다.

1. 어휘 수준과 문장의 난이도, 분량 등 국내 영어 학습자들에게 적합한 정도를 종합적으로 검토하여 선정하였습니다.
2. 기존 원서 독자층 사이의 인기도까지 감안하여 최적의 작품들을 선별하였습니다.
3. 판형이 좁고 글씨가 작아 읽기 힘들었던 원서 디자인을 대폭 수정하여, 판형을 시원하게 키우고 읽기에 최적화된 영문 서체를 사용하여 가독성을 극대화하였습니다.
4. 함께 제공되는 워크북은 어려운 어휘를 완벽하게 정리하고 이해력을 점검하는 퀴즈를 덧붙여 독자들이 원서를 보다 쉽고 재미있게 읽을 수 있도록 구성하였습니다.
5. 기존에 높은 가격에 판매되어 구입이 부담스러웠던 오디오북을 부록으로 제공하여 리스닝과 소리 내어 읽기에까지 원서를 두루 활용할 수 있도록 했습니다.

루이스 새커(Louis Sachar)는 현재 미국에서 가장 인기 있는 아동 문학 작가 중 한 사람입니다. 그는 1954년 미국 뉴욕에서 태어났으며 초등학교 보조 교사로 일한 경험을 바탕으로 쓴 「Wayside School」 시리즈로 잘 알려져 있습니다. 그 외에도 그는 「Marvin Redpost」 시리즈, 「There's a Boy in the Girls' Bathroom」, 「The Boy Who Lost His Face」 등 20여 권의 어린이책을 썼습니다. 그가 1998년에 발표한 「Holes」는 독자들의 큰 사랑을 받으며 전미도서상 등 많은 상을 수상하였고, 마침내 1999년에는 뉴베리 메달을 수상하였습니다. 2006년에는 「Holes」의 후속편 「Small Steps」를 출간하였습니다.

「There's a Boy in the Girls' Bathroom」은 모두에게 미움 받는 아이 Bradley의 이야기를 담고 있습니다. Bradley는 숙제도 하지 않고 시험에서는 늘 F를 받는, 학교에서 알아주는 문제아입니다. 그는 틈만 나면 거짓말을 하고 문제를 일으킵니다. 친구들은 물론 선생님들 조차 그를 싫어하며 그에게 가까이 가려 하지 않습니다. 그런 그에게 학교에 새로 전근 온 카운슬러 Carla가 다가옵니다. Bradley는 처음에 Carla와의 상담을 거부하지만 점차 그녀에게 마음을 열게 됩니다.
모두가 싫어하고 모두를 싫어하는 문제아 Bradley는 이렇게 조금씩 세상과 소통하는 방법, 그리고 자기 자신을 사랑하게 되는 방법을 배워갑니다.

원서 본문

내용이 담긴 원서 본문입니다.
원어민이 읽는 일반 원서와 같은 텍스트지만, 암기해야 할 중요 어휘들은 볼드체로 표시되어 있습니다. 이 어휘들은 지금 들고 계신 워크북에 챕터별로 정리되어 있습니다.

학습 심리학 연구 결과에 따르면, 한 단어씩 따로 외우는 단어 암기는 거의 효과가 없다고 합니다. 단어를 제대로 외우기 위해서는 문맥(context) 속에서 단어를 암기해야 하며, 한 단어당 문맥 속에서 15번 이상 마주칠 때 완벽하게 암기할 수 있다고 합니다.

이 책의 본문에서는 중요 어휘를 볼드체로 강조하여, 문맥 속의 단어들을 더 확실히 인지(word cognition in context)하도록 돕고 있습니다. 또한 대부분의 중요 단어들은 다른 챕터에서도 반복해서 등장하기 때문에 이 책을 읽는 것만으로도 자연스럽게 어휘력을 향상시킬 수 있습니다.

또한 본문 하단에는 내용 이해를 돕기 위한 '각주'가 첨가되어 있습니다. 각주는 굳이 암기할 필요는 없지만, 알아 두면 도움이 될 만한 정보를 설명하고 있습니다. 각주를 참고하면 스토리를 더 깊이 있게 이해할 수 있어 원서를 읽는 재미가 배가됩니다.

워크북(Workbook)

Check Your Reading Speed

해당 챕터의 단어 수가 기록되어 있어, 리딩 속도를 측정할 수 있습니다. 특히 리딩 속도를 중시하는 독자들이 유용하게 사용할 수 있습니다.

Build Your Vocabulary

본문에 볼드 표시되어 있던 단어들이 정리되어 있습니다. 리딩 전, 후에 반복해서 보면 원서를 더욱 쉽게 읽을 수 있고, 어휘력도 빠르게 향상될 것입니다.

단어는 〈스펠링 – 빈도 – 발음기호 – 품사 – 한글 뜻 – 영문 뜻〉 순서로 표기되어 있으며 빈도 표시(★)가 많을수록 필수 어휘입니다. 반복해서 등장하는 단어는 빈도 대신 '복습'으로 표기되어 있습니다. 품사는 아래와 같이 표기했습니다.

n. 명사 | a. 형용사 | ad. 부사 | v. 동사
conj. 접속사 | prep. 전치사 | int. 감탄사 | idiom 숙어 및 관용구

Comprehension Quiz

간단한 퀴즈를 통해 읽은 내용에 대한 이해력을 점검해 볼 수 있습니다.

이 책의 활용법

「뉴베리 컬렉션」 이렇게 읽어 보세요!

아래와 같이 프리뷰(Preview) → 리딩(Reading) → 리뷰(Review) 세 단계를 거치면서 읽으면, 더욱 효과적으로 영어 실력을 향상할 수 있습니다!

1. 프리뷰(Preview) : 오늘 읽을 내용을 먼저 점검하자!

- 워크북을 통해 오늘 읽을 챕터에 나와 있는 단어들을 쭉 훑어봅니다. 어떤 단어들이 나오는지, 내가 아는 단어와 모르는 단어가 어떤 것들이 있는지 가벼운 마음으로 살펴봅니다.
- 평소처럼 하나하나 쓰면서 암기하려고 하지는 마세요! 익숙하지 않은 단어들을 주의 깊게 보되, 어차피 리딩을 하면서 점차 익숙해질 단어라는 것을 기억하며 빠르게 훑어봅니다.
- 뒤 챕터로 갈수록 '복습'이라고 표시된 단어들이 늘어나는 것을 알 수 있습니다. '복습' 단어인데도 여전히 익숙하지 않다면 더욱 신경을 써서 봐야겠죠? 매일매일 꾸준히 읽는다면, 익숙한 단어들이 점점 많아진다는 것을 몸으로 느낄 수 있습니다.

2. 리딩(Reading) : 내용에 집중하며 빠르게 읽어 나가자!

- 프리뷰를 마친 후 바로 리딩을 시작합니다. 방금 살펴봤던 어휘들을 문장 속에서 다시 만나게 되는데 이 과정에서 단어의 쓰임새와 어감을 자연스럽게 익히게 됩니다.
- 모르는 단어나 이해되지 않는 문장이 나오더라도 멈추지 말고 전체적인 맥락을 잡아가면서 속도감 있게 읽어 나가세요. 이해되지 않는 문장들은 따로 표시를 하되, 일단 넘어가고 계속 읽는 것이 좋습니다. 뒷부분을 읽다 보면 자연히 이해가 되는 경우도 있고, 정 이해가 되지 않는 부분은 리딩을 마친 이후에 따로 리뷰하는 시간을 가지면 됩니다. 문제집을 풀듯이 모든 문장을 분석하면서 원서를 읽는 것이 아니라, 리딩을 할 때는 리딩에만, 리뷰를 할 때는 리뷰에만 집중하는 것이 필요합니다.
- 볼드 처리된 단어의 의미가 궁금하더라도 워크북을 바로 펼치지 마세요. 정 궁금하다면 한 번씩 참고하는 것도 나쁘진 않지만, 워크북과 원서를 번갈아 보면서 읽는 것은 리딩의 흐름을 끊고 단어 하나하나에 집착하는 좋지 않은 리딩 습관을 심어 줄 수 있습니다.
- 같은 맥락에서 번역서를 구해 원서와 동시에 번갈아 보는 것도 좋은 방법이 아닙니다. 한글 번역을 가지고 있다고 해도 일단 영어로 읽을 때는 영어에만 집중하고 어느 정도 분량을 읽은 후에 번역서와 비교하도록 하세요. 모든 문장을 일일이 번역해서 완벽하게 이해하려는 것은 오히려 좋지 않은 리딩 습관을 심

10

어 주어 장기직으로는 바람직하지 않은 결과를 입을 수 있습니다. 처음부터 완벽하게 이해하려고 하는 것보다는 빠른 속도로 2~3회 반복해서 읽는 방식이 실력 향상에 더 도움이 됩니다. 만일 반복해서 읽어도 내용이 전혀 이해되지 않아 곤란하다면 책 선정에 문제가 있다고 할 수 있습니다. 그럴 때는 좀 더 쉬운 책을 골라 실력을 다진 뒤 다시 도전하는 것이 좋습니다.

• 초보자라면 분당 150단어의 리딩 속도를 목표로 잡고 리딩을 합니다. 분당 150단어는 원어민이 말하는 속도로, 영어 학습자들이 리스닝과 스피킹으로 넘어가기 위해 가장 기초적으로 달성해야 하는 단계입니다. 분당 50~80단어 정도의 낮은 리딩 속도를 가지고 있는 경우는 대부분 영어 실력이 부족해서라기보다 '잘못된 리딩 습관'을 가지고 있어서 그렇습니다. 이해력이 조금 떨어진다고 하더라도 분당 150단어까지는 속도에 대한 긴장감을 놓치지 말고 속도감 있게 읽어 나가도록 하세요.

3. 리뷰(Review) : 이해력을 점검하고 꼼꼼하게 다시 살펴보자!

• 해당 챕터의 Comprehension Quiz를 통해 이해력을 점검해 봅니다.
• 오늘 만난 어휘들을 다시 한번 복습합니다. 이때는 읽으면서 중요하다고 생각했던 단어를 연습장에 써 보면서 꼼꼼하게 외우는 것도 좋습니다.
• 이해가 되지 않는다고 표시해 두었던 부분도 주의 깊게 분석해 봅니다. 다시 한번 문장을 꼼꼼히 읽고, 어떤 이유에서 이해가 되지 않았는지 생각해 봅니다. 따로 메모를 남기거나 노트를 작성하는 것도 좋은 방법입니다.
• 사실 꼼꼼히 리뷰하는 것은 매우 고된 과정입니다. 원서를 읽고 리뷰하는 시간을 가지는 것이 영어 실력 향상에 많은 도움이 되기는 하지만, 이 과정을 철저히 지키려다가 원서 읽기의 재미를 반감시키는 것은 바람직하지 않습니다. 그럴 때는 차라리 리뷰를 가볍게 하는 것이 좋을 수 있습니다. '내용에 빠져서 재미있게', 문제집에서는 상상도 못할 '많은 양'을 읽으면서, 매일매일 조금씩 꾸준히 실력을 키워가는 것이 원서를 활용하는 기본적인 방법이며, 영어 공부의 왕도입니다. 문제집 풀듯이 원서 읽기를 시도하고 접근해서는 실패할 수밖에 없습니다.
• 이런 방식으로 원서를 끝까지 다 읽었다면, 다시 반복해서 읽거나 오디오북을 활용하는 등 다양한 방식으로 원서 읽기를 확장해 나갈 수 있습니다. 이에 대한 자세한 안내가 워크북 말미에 실려 있습니다.

1. Where did Bradley Chalkers sit in class?
   A. He sat at a desk in the first row of the room.
   B. He sat at a desk in the last row of the room.
   C. He sat next to the teacher's desk.
   D. He sat in the closet.

2. Why did Jeff give a dollar to Bradley?
   A. Bradley looked poor and Jeff pitied him.
   B. Bradley said that he would beat him up.
   C. Bradley said that he would spit on him.
   D. Bradley said that he would do his homework.

3. Why did Bradley give the dollar back to Jeff?
   A. He said he was rich and didn't need it.
   B. He wanted Jeff to tell him about Washington, D.C.
   C. He wanted Jeff to have money for lunch.
   D. He wanted Jeff to be his friend.

4. Who did Bradley talk to in his room?
   A. His collection of animals
   B. His online friends
   C. His sister, Claudia
   D. His video games

5. Why had Mrs. Ebbel called Bradley's mother?
   A. She called to tell her about Parents' Conference Day.
   B. She called to tell her about Bradley's new friend.
   C. She called to tell her about Bradley's good grades.
   D. She called to tell her about Bradley becoming class president.

6. What had happened to Bradley's father on his job with the police?
   A. He had been beaten up by a criminal.
   B. He had been fired for shooting a robber.
   C. He had been shot in the arm chasing a robber.
   D. He had been shot in the leg chasing a robber.

7. How did Carla feel about Bradley before they met?
   A. She thought he sounded horrible and didn't want to meet him.
   B. She thought he sounded charming and wanted to meet him.
   C. She thought that he sounded like a normal student.
   D. She hadn't heard anything at all about Bradley.

1분에 몇 단어를 읽는지 리딩 속도를 측정해보세요.

$$\frac{656 \text{ words}}{\text{reading time ( ) sec}} \times 60 = (\quad) \text{ WPM}$$

Build Your Vocabulary

row**
[rou]

① n. 열, 줄 ② v. 노를 젓다, 배를 젓다; n. 노 젓기
A row of things or people is a number of them arranged in a line.

closet*
[klázit]

n. 옷장, 벽장
A closet is a piece of furniture with doors at the front and shelves inside, which is used for storing things.

all in all

idiom 전반적으로 보아, 대체로
All in all refers to when everything is considered.

unfortunate*
[ʌnfɔ́:rtʃənət]

a. 불운한, 불행한 (unfortunately ad. 불행하게도, 유감스럽게도)
If you describe someone as unfortunate, you mean that something unpleasant or unlucky has happened to them.

fit***
[fit]

v. (모양·크기가 어떤 사람·사물에) 맞다; 끼우다; 적절하다
If something fits, it is the right size and shape to go onto a person's body or onto a particular object.

capital**
[kǽpətl]

n. 수도, 중심지; 자본, 자산; a. 자본의; 주요한
The capital of a country is the city or town where its government or parliament meets.

urge*
[ə:rdʒ]

v. 촉구하다, 충고하다, 재촉하다; n. (강한) 충동
If you urge someone to do something, you try hard to persuade them to do it.

shrug*
[ʃrʌg]

v. (양 손바닥을 내보이면서 어깨를) 으쓱하다; n. 으쓱하기
If you shrug, you raise your shoulders to show that you are not interested in something or that you do not know or care about something.

mumble
[mʌmbl]

v. 중얼거리다, 웅얼거리다; n. 중얼거림
If you mumble, you speak very quietly and not at all clearly with the result that the words are difficult to understand.

exclaim*
[ikskléim]

v. 외치다, 소리치다
If you exclaim, you say or shout something suddenly because of surprise, fear and pleasure.

frown*
[fraun]

v. 얼굴을 찡그리다, 눈살을 찌푸리다; n. 찌푸린 얼굴
When someone frowns, their eyebrows become drawn together, because they are annoyed or puzzled.

14

stretch**
[streʧ]

v. 늘이다; 늘어지다; 기지개를 켜다; (팔 · 다리의 근육을) 당기다; n. 기지개 켜기
When something soft or elastic stretches or is stretched, it becomes longer or bigger as well as thinner, usually because it is pulled.

stare*
[stɛər]

v. 응시하다, 뚫어지게 보다
If you stare at someone or something, you look at them for a long time.

bulge
[bʌldʒ]

v. 툭 튀어 나오다, 부풀어 오르다; n. 불룩한 것 (bulging a. 튀어 나온)
If something such as a person's stomach bulges, it sticks out.

awkward**
[ɔ́:kwərd]

a. 어색한, 불편한, 곤란한 (awkwardly ad. 어색하게, 거북하게)
Someone who feels awkward behaves in a shy or embarrassed way.

scribble
[skribl]

v. 낙서하다; 갈겨쓰다; 휘갈기다; n. 낙서
To scribble means to make meaningless marks or rough drawings using a pencil or pen.

tape*
[teip]

v. (접착) 테이프로 붙이다; 녹음하다, 녹화하다;
n. (소리 · 영상을 기록하는) 테이프; (접착용) 테이프
If you tape one thing to another, you attach it using sticky strip of plastic.

gob
[gab]

n. 많은 양
Gobs of something is a large amount or quantity of it.

junk*
[dʒʌŋk]

n. 쓸모 없는 물건, 쓰레기
Junk is old and used goods that have little value and that you do not want any more.

sharpen*
[ʃá:rpən]

v. 날카롭게 하다, (날카롭게) 갈다
If you sharpen an object, you make its edge very thin or you make its end pointed.

wad
[wad]

n. 뭉치, 다발
A wad of something such as paper or cloth is a tight bundle or ball of it.

tear**
[tɛər]

① v. (tore-torn) 찢다, 찢어지다; 부리나케 가다; n. 찢음 ② n. 눈물
If you tear paper, cloth, or another material, or if it tears, you pull it into two pieces or you pull it so that a hole appears in it.

chew*
[ʧuː]

v. 씹다, 씹어서 으깨다
If a person or animal chews an object, they bite it with their teeth.

erase*
[iréis]

v. (지우개 등으로) 지우다; (완전히) 지우다, 없애다 (eraser n. 지우개)
If you erase something such as writing or a mark, you remove it, usually by rubbing it with an eraser.

recognizable
[rékəgnàizəbl]

a. 인식할 수 있는, 알아볼 수 있는 (unrecognizable a. 인식할 수 없는)
If something can be easily recognized or identified, you can say that it is easily recognizable.

stuff*
[stʌf]

n. 것(들), 물건, 물질; v. 채워 넣다, 속을 채우다
You can use stuff to refer to things such as a substance, a collection of things, events, or ideas in a general way without mentioning the thing itself by name.

distort
[distɔ́ːrt]

v. (얼굴 등을) 찡그리다, 찌푸리다; 비틀다; 왜곡하다
(distorted a. 찌그러진, 일그러진)
If someone's face or body distorts or is distorted, it moves into an unnatural and unattractive shape or position.

scissors[*]
[sízərz]

n. 가위
Scissors are a small cutting tool with two sharp blades that are screwed together.

tiny[**]
[táini]

a. 몹시 작은
Something or someone that is tiny is extremely small.

recess[*]
[ríːses]

n. (학교의) 쉬는 시간; 휴회
A recess is a short period of time when you have a rest or a change from what you are doing, especially if you are working or if you are in a boring or unpleasant situation.

startle[*]
[stáːrtl]

v. 깜짝 놀라게 하다; 움찔하다; n. 깜짝 놀람 (startled a. 깜짝 놀란)
If something sudden and unexpected startles you, it surprises and frightens you slightly.

alongside[*]
[əlɔ́ːŋsáid]

prep. ~옆에, 나란히
If one thing is alongside another thing, the first thing is next to the second.

amaze[*]
[əméiz]

v. 깜짝 놀라게 하다 (amazement n. 놀람, 경탄)
If something amazes you, it surprises you very much.

admit[***]
[ædmít]

v. 인정하다
If you admit that something bad, unpleasant, or embarrassing is true, you agree, often unwillingly, that it is true.

spit[*]
[spit]

v. (침 등을) 뱉다; 내뱉듯이 말하다; n. 침
If someone spits, they force an amount of liquid out of their mouth, often to show hatred or contemp.

Check Your Reading Speed

1분에 몇 단어를 읽는지 리딩 속도를 측정해보세요.

$$\frac{620 \text{ words}}{\text{reading time ( ) sec}} \times 60 = (\quad) \text{ WPM}$$

Build Your Vocabulary

spit^{복습}
[spit]

v. (침 등을) 뱉다; 내뱉듯이 말하다; n. 침 (spitter n. 침 뱉는 사람)
If someone spits, they force an amount of liquid out of their mouth, often to show hatred or contemp.

describe**
[diskráib]

v. 묘사하다, 기술하다; 평하다
If you describe a person, object, event, or situation, you say what they are like or what happened.

grade**
[greid]

n. 학년, 등급; 성적, 평점; v. 점수를 매기다, 등급을 매기다
In the United States, a grade is a group of classes in which all the children are of a similar age.

stare^{복습}
[stɛər]

v. 응시하다, 뚫어지게 보다
If you stare at someone or something, you look at them for a long time.

recess^{복습}
[ri:ses]

n. (학교의) 쉬는 시간; 휴회
A recess is a short period of time when you have a rest or a change from what you are doing, especially if you are working or if you are in a boring or unpleasant situation.

figure***
[fígjər]

v. 생각하다, 판단하다; 계산하다; n. 계산, 모습, 인물
If you figure that something is the case, you think or guess that it is the case.

tell on

idiom ～을 일러바치다
If you tell on someone, you tell a teacher or prerson in authority that they have done something wrong.

row^{복습}
[rou]

① n. 열, 줄 ② v. 노를 젓다, 배를 젓다; n. 노 젓기
A row of things or people is a number of them arranged in a line.

punch*
[pʌntʃ]

v. 주먹으로 치다, 때리다; n. 주먹으로 한 대 침, 펀치
If you punch someone or something, you hit them hard with your fist.

glare*
[glɛər]

v. 노려보다; 번쩍번쩍 빛나다; n. 노려봄; 섬광
If you glare at someone, you look at them with an angry expression on your face.

sigh*
[sai]

v. 한숨 쉬다; n. 한숨, 탄식
When you sigh, you let out a deep breath, as a way of expressing feelings such as disappointment, tiredness, or pleasure.

steal***
[sti:l]

v. (stole-stolen) 훔치다, 도둑질하다
If you steal something from someone, you take it away from them without their permission and without intending to return it.

eye*
[ai]

v. (탐이 나거나 의심스러워) 쳐다보다; n. 눈
If you eye someone or something in a particular way, you look at them carefully in that way.

suspicious*
[səspíʃəs]

a. 의심하는, 수상쩍은 (suspiciously ad. 의심스러운 듯이)
If you are suspicious of someone or something, you do not trust them, and are careful when dealing with them.

conference*
[kánfərəns]

n. 회담, 회의, 협의
A conference is a meeting, often lasting a few days, which is organized on a particular subject or to bring together people who have a common interest.

hire*
[haiər]

v. 고용하다; 빌리다, 빌려주다; n. 고용
If you hire someone, you employ them or pay them to do a particular job for you.

counsel*
[káunsəl]

v. 상담을 하다; n. 조언, 충고 (counselor n. 지도교사, 상담사)
If you counsel people, you give them advice about their problems.

bowling alley
[bóuliŋ æli]

n. 볼링장
A bowling alley is a building which contains several tracks for bowling.

let the matter drop

idiom 문제를 보류하다
If you let the matter drop, you do or say nothing more about it.

glance*
[glæns]

v. 흘긋 보다, 잠깐 보다; n. 흘긋 봄
If you glance at something or someone, you look at them very quickly and then look away again immediately.

scribble^{복습}
[skríbl]

v. 낙서하다; 갈겨쓰다, 휘갈기다; n. 낙서
To scribble means to make meaningless marks or rough drawings using a pencil or pen.

confuse**
[kənfjúːz]

v. 어리둥절하게 하다, 혼동하다
To confuse someone means to make it difficult for them to know exactly what is happening or what to do.

bother*
[báðər]

v. 귀찮게 하다, 괴롭히다; 일부러 ~하다, 애를 쓰다
If someone bothers you, they talk to you when you want to be left alone or interrupt you when you are busy.

threaten**
[θretn]

v. 위협하다, 협박하다; 조짐을 보이다
If a person threatens to do something unpleasant to you, or if they threaten you, they say or imply that they will do something unpleasant to you, especially if you do not do what they want.

bang*
[bæŋ]

v. 부딪치다; 탕 치다, 쾅 닫다; n. 쾅 하는 소리
If you bang on something or if you bang it, you hit it hard, making a loud noise.

catch up

idiom 따라잡다, 따라가다
If you catch up with someone, you reach them by walking faster than them.

grab*
[græb]

v. 부여잡다, 움켜쥐다; n. 부여잡기
If you grab something, you take it or pick it up suddenly and roughly.

18

twist**
[twist]

v. 비틀다, 돌리다, 꼬다; n. 뒤틀림; 엉킴 (twisted a. 비뚤어진)

If you twist something, especially a part of your body, or if it twists, it moves into an unusual, uncomfortable, or bent position, for example because of being hit or pushed, or because you are upset.

1분에 몇 단어를 읽는지 리딩 속도를 측정해보세요.

$$\frac{1{,}767 \text{ words}}{\text{reading time (}\quad\text{) sec}} \times 60 = (\quad) \text{ WPM}$$

Build Your Vocabulary

make a face idiom 얼굴을 찌푸리다
If you make a face, you twist your face to indicate a certain mental or emotional state.

sleeve*
[sli:v]
n. (옷의) 소매, 소맷자락 (sleeveless a. 소매가 없는)
The sleeves of a coat, shirt, or other item of clothing are the parts that cover your arms.

butcher*
[bútʃər]
n. 정육점 주인; 도살업자; v. 도살하다, 학살하다 (butcher knife n. 육류용 칼)
A butcher is a shopkeeper who cuts up and sells meat.

race
[reis]
① v. 질주하다, 달리다; 경주하다; n. 경주 ② n. 인종, 민족
If you race somewhere, you go there as quickly as possible.

lie***
[lai]
① v. (lay-lain) 놓여 있다, 위치하다; 눕다, 누워 있다 ② v. 거짓말하다; n. 거짓말
If an object lies in a particular place, it is in a flat position in that place.

counter*
[káuntər]
n. (부엌의) 조리대; 계산대; 긴 테이블; v. 반박하다
A counter is a flat surface in a kitchen which is easy to clean and on which you can prepare food.

hack
[hæk]
v. 마구 자르다, 난도질하다; 해킹하다
If you hack something or hack at it, you cut it with strong, rough strokes using a sharp tool such as an ax or knife.

hall***
[hɔːl]
n. (건물 입구 안쪽의) 현관; (건물 안의) 복도
The hall in a house or flat is the area just inside the front door, into which some of the other rooms open.

announce**
[ənáuns]
v. 발표하다, 알리다
If you announce a piece of news or an intention, especially something that people may not like, you say it loudly and clearly, so that everyone you are with can hear it.

pretend***
[priténd]
v. ~인 체하다, 가장하다; a. 가짜의, 꾸민
If you pretend that something is the case, you act in a way that is intended to make people believe that it is the case, although in fact it is not.

collect***
[kəlékt]
v. 모으다, 수집하다 (collection n. 수집품, 소장품)
If you collect a number of things, you bring them together from several places or from several people.

brass*
[bræs]
n. 놋쇠, 황동
Brass is a yellow-colored metal made from copper and zinc.

20

garbage*
[gárbidʒ]

n. 쓰레기 (garbage can n. 쓰레기통)
Garbage is rubbish, especially waste from a kitchen.

ivory*
[áivəri]

a. 상아로 만든; 상아색의; n. 상아
An ivory thing is made of a hard cream-colored substance which forms the tusks of elephants.

donkey*
[dánki]

n. [동물] 당나귀
A donkey is an animal which is like a horse but which is smaller and has longer ears.

owl*
[aul]

n. [동물] 올빼미
An owl is a bird with a flat face, large eyes, and a small sharp beak. Most owls obtain their food by hunting small animals at night.

horn*
[hɔːrn]

n. 뿔; (자동차 등의) 경적
The horns of an animal such as a cow or deer are the hard pointed things that grow from its head.

attach*
[ətǽtʃ]

v. 붙이다, 부착하다
If you attach something to an object, you connect it or fasten it to the object.

ashtray
[ǽʃtrèi]

n. 재떨이
An ashtray is a container into which people who smoke put ash or cigarette ends.

raccoon*
[rækúːn]

n. [동물] 너구리
A raccoon is a small animal that has dark-colored fur with white stripes on its face and on its long tail.

chip**
[tʃip]

v. 깨지다, 이가 빠지다; 잘게 썰다; n. 조각, 토막
If you chip something or if it chips, a small piece is broken off it.

go off

idiom (무엇을 하러) 자리를 뜨다; 폭발하다
If you go off, you leave a place, especially in order to do something.

lean**
[liːn]

v. 기울다, 기울이다, (몸을) 숙이다; ~에 기대다; ~을 ~에 기대 놓다
When you lean in a particular direction, you bend your body in that direction.

pillow*
[pílou]

n. 베개
A pillow is a rectangular cushion which you rest your head on when you are in bed.

demand***
[dimǽnd]

v. 묻다, 요구하다, 청구하다; n. 요구, 수요
If you demand something such as information or action, you ask for it in a very forceful way.

giggle*
[gigl]

v. 킬킬 웃다; n. 킬킬 웃음
If someone giggles, they laugh in a childlike way, because they are amused, nervous, or embarrassed.

tiny ^{복습}
[táini]

a. 몹시 작은
Something or someone that is tiny is extremely small.

glue*
[gluː]

v. 풀로 붙이다, 접착하다; n. 풀, 접착제
If you glue one object to another, you stick them together using glue.

ceramic
[sərǽmik]

a. 도자기의; n. 도자기
A ceramic thing is made of clay that has been heated to a very high temperature to become hard.

hind*
[haind]

a. 뒤쪽의, 후방의
An animal's hind legs are at the back of its body.

reveal*
[rivíːl]

v. 드러내다, 보이다, 나타내다
If you reveal something that has been out of sight, you uncover it so that people can see it.

tongue**
[tʌŋ]

n. 혀
Your tongue is the soft movable part inside your mouth which you use for tasting, eating, and speaking.

make out

idiom (~와) 키스하다; 성공하다
To make out with someone means to kiss and touch them in a sexual way.

scold*
[skould]

v. 꾸짖다, 잔소리하다
If you scold someone, you speak angrily to them because they have done something wrong.

handful*
[hǽndfùl]

n. 한 움큼, 손에 그득, 한 줌
A handful of something is the amount of it that you can hold in your hand.

cut something up

idiom ~을 조각조각[잘게] 자르다 (cut-up a. 조각조각 잘린)
If you cut something up, you divide something into small pieces with a knife or a tool.

scoop
[skuːp]

v. 재빨리 들어 올리다; 뜨다, 파다; n. 국자, 주걱
If you scoop a person or thing somewhere, you put your hands or arms under or round them and quickly move them there.

let's hear it for

idiom ~에 성원을 보냅시다
People say 'let's hear it for' to cheer and applaud someone who deserves a lot of praise.

cheer**
[ʧiər]

v. 환호성을 지르다, 응원하다; n. 환호(성)
When people cheer, they shout loudly to show their approval or to encourage someone who is doing something such as taking part in a game.

hop*
[hap]

v. 깡충 뛰다, 뛰어오르다; n. 깡충깡충 뜀
If you hop, you move along by jumping.

pond*
[pand]

n. (주로 인공적인) 연못
A pond is a small area of water that is smaller than a lake.

stain*
[stein]

n. 얼룩, 오점; v. 더러워지다, 얼룩지게 하다
If a liquid stains something, the thing becomes colored or marked by the liquid.

bedspread
[bédsprèd]

n. 침대보
A bedspread is a decorative cover which is put over a bed, on top of the sheets and blankets.

spill*
[spil]

v. 엎지르다, 흘리다; n. 엎지름, 유출
If a liquid spills or if you spill it, it accidentally flows over the edge of a container.

cramp
[kræmp]

n. 경련, 쥐; v. 경련을 일으키다
Cramp is a sudden strong pain caused by a muscle suddenly contracting.

remind**
[rimáind]

v. 생각나게 하다, 상기시키다, 일깨우다
If someone reminds you of a fact or event that you already know about, they say something which makes you think about it.

drown*
[draun]

v. 물에 빠져 죽다, 익사하다
When someone drowns or is drowned, they die because they have gone or been pushed under water and cannot breathe.

rescue*
[réskju:]

v. 구조하다, 구출하다; n. 구출, 구원
If you rescue someone, you get them out of a dangerous or unpleasant situation.

hold on

idiom 기다려
You say 'hold on' to ask someone to wait or stop for a short time.

swing**
[swiŋ]

v. (swung–swung) (한 점을 축으로 하여) 빙 돌다, 휙 움직이다; 휘두르다
If something swings in a particular direction or if you swing it in that direction, it moves in that direction with a smooth, curving movement.

barge in

idiom 불쑥 들어오다, 불쑥 끼어들다
To barge in means to enter a place or join a group of people quickly and rudely, without being asked.

snap*
[snæp]

v. (화난 목소리로) 딱딱거리다; 딱[툭] (하고) 부러뜨리다, 부러지다
If someone snaps at you, they speak to you in a sharp, unfriendly way.

punch복습
[pʌntʃ]

v. 주먹으로 치다, 때리다; n. 주먹으로 한 대 침, 펀치
If you punch someone or something, you hit them hard with your fist.

tease*
[ti:z]

v. 놀리다, 장난하다; n. 장난, 놀림
To tease someone means to laugh at them or make jokes about them in order to embarrass, annoy, or upset them.

brace*
[breis]

n. (pl.) 치열 교정기; 버팀대; v. (스스로) 대비를 하다
A brace is a metal device that can be fastened to a child's teeth in order to help them grow straight.

accidental*
[æksədéntl]

a. 우연한; 부수적인 (accidentally ad. 우연히)
An accidental event happens by chance or as the result of an accident, and is not deliberately intended.

strew
[stru:]

v. (strewed–strewn) 뿌리다, 흩뿌리다
If a place is strewn with things, they are lying scattered there.

desert**
[dézərt]

① n. 사막, 황무지 ② v. 버리다, 유기하다; 인적이 끊기다
A desert is a large area of land, usually in a hot region, where there is almost no water, rain, trees, or plants.

insist**
[insíst]

v. 우기다, 주장하다; 강요하다
If you insist that something is the case, you say so very firmly and refuse to say otherwise, even though other people do not believe you.

arrange**
[əréindʒ]

v. 가지런히 하다, 배열하다; 준비하다
If you arrange things somewhere, you place them in a particular position, usually in order to make them look attractive or tidy.

alphabetical*
[ælfəbétikəl]

a. 알파벳순의
Alphabetical means arranged according to the normal order of the letters in the alphabet.

snicker
[sníkər]

v. 킬킬 웃다, 숨죽여 웃다; n. 킬킬 웃음
If you snicker, you laugh quietly in a disrespectful way, for example at something rude or embarrassing.

make fun of

idiom ~을 놀리다, 웃음거리로 만들다
If you make fun of someone, you make unkind remarks or jokes them.

make up for

idiom ~에 대해 보상하다, (잘못된 상황을 바로잡을 수 있도록) 만회하다
If you make up for something, you do something good for someone because you have treated them badly or because they have done something good for you.

stove*
[stouv]

n. (요리용) 화로, 레인지; 스토브, 난로; v. 난로로 데우다
A stove is a piece of equipment which provides heat, either for cooking or for heating a room.

elect***
[ilékt]

v. 선거하다, 선출하다
When people elect someone, they choose that person to represent them, by voting for them.

grade 복습
[greid]

n. 성적, 평점; 학년, 등급; v. 점수를 매기다, 등급을 매기다
Your grade in an examination or piece of written work is the mark you get, usually in the form of a letter or number, which indicates your level of achievement.

flutter*
[flʌ́tər]

v. (깃발 등이) 펄럭이다, (새 등이) 날갯짓하다; n. 펄럭임
If something thin or light flutters, or if you flutter it, it moves up and down or from side to side with a lot of quick, light movements.

conference 복습
[kánfərəns]

n. 회담, 회의, 협의
A conference is a meeting, often lasting a few days, which is organized on a particular subject or to bring together people who have a common interest.

innocent*
[ínəsənt]

a. 순진한; 잘못이 없는, 결백한 (innocently ad. 순진하게)
If someone is innocent, they have no experience or knowledge of the more complex or unpleasant aspects of life.

appointment**
[əpɔ́intmənt]

n. 약속, 예약; 지정, 임명
If you have an appointment with someone, you have arranged to see them at a particular time, usually in connection with their work or for a serious purpose.

24

disbelief*
[dìsbilí:f]

n. 믿기지 않음, 불신감
Disbelief is not believing that something is true or real.

stamp**
[stæmp]

v. (발을) 구르다, 짓밟다; (도장 · 스탬프 등을) 찍다; n. 우표, 인지; 도장
If you stamp or stamp your foot, you lift your foot and put it down very hard on the ground, for example because you are angry.

slam*
[slæm]

v. (문을) 탕 닫다, 세게 치다; 털썩 내려놓다; n. 쾅 (하는 소리)
If you slam a door or window or if it slams, it shuts noisily and with great force.

knock**
[nak]

v. (문을) 두드리다, 노크하다; 치다, 부수다; n. 노크; 타격
If you knock on something such as a door or window, you hit it, usually several times, to attract someone's attention.

yell*
[jel]

v. 소리치다, 고함치다; n. 고함소리, 부르짖음
If you yell, you shout loudly, usually because you are excited, angry, or in pain.

chase**
[tʃeis]

v. 뒤쫓다; 추구하다; 쫓아내다; n. 추적, 추격
If you chase someone, or chase after them, you run after them or follow them quickly in order to catch or reach them.

robber*
[rábər]

n. 강도, 도둑
A robber is someone who steals money or property from a bank, a shop, or a vehicle, often by using force or threats.

cane*
[kein]

n. 지팡이
A cane is a long thin stick with a curved or round top which you can use to support yourself when you are walking.

grumpy
[grʌ́mpi]

a. 성미 까다로운, 심술난
If you say that someone is grumpy, you mean that they are bad-tempered and miserable.

short-tempered
[ʃɔ́:rt-témpərd]

a. 성급한
Someone who is short-tempered gets angry very quickly.

stick**
[stik]

① v. 붙이다, 달라붙다; 찔러 넣다, 찌르다; 내밀다 ② n. 막대기, 지팡이
If one thing sticks to another, it becomes attached to it and is difficult to remove.

throw up

idiom ～을 토하다, 게우다
When someone throws up, they bring food they have eaten back out of mouth.

plate**
[pleit]

n. 접시, 그릇
A plate is a round or oval flat dish that is used to hold food.

nonsense**
[nánsens]

n. 허튼소리; 바보 같은 짓; a. 어리석은, 무의미한
If you say that something spoken or written is nonsense, you mean that you consider it to be untrue or silly.

exclaim복습
[ikskléim]

v. 외치다, 소리치다
If you exclaim, you say or shout something suddenly because of surprise, fear and pleasure.

protest[prətést]
v. 항의하다, 이의를 제기하다; n. 항의
If you protest against something or about something, you say or show publicly that you object to it.

accuse[əkjúːz]
v. 비난하다, 고발하다
If you accuse someone of doing something wrong or dishonest, you say or tell them that you believe that they did it.

glare[glɛər]
v. 노려보다; 번쩍번쩍 빛나다; n. 노려봄; 섬광
If you glare at someone, you look at them with an angry expression on your face.

feed[fiːd]
v. 먹이를 주다, 음식을 먹이다; 공급하다
If you feed a person or animal, you give them food to eat and sometimes actually put it in their mouths.

flabbergast[flǽbərgæst]
v. 소스라쳐 놀라게 하다, 당황하게 하다 (flabbergasted a. 놀란, 당황스러운)
If you say that you are flabbergasted, you are emphasizing that you are extremely surprised.

tolerate[tálərèit]
v. 참다, 견디다; 관대히 다루다, 묵인하다
If you can tolerate something unpleasant or painful, you are able to bear it.

rage[reidʒ]
n. 격렬한 분노; v. 몹시 화를 내다; (폭풍·전투·언쟁 등이) 맹렬히 계속되다
Rage is strong anger that is difficult to control.

liar[laiər]
n. 거짓말쟁이
If you say that someone is a liar, you mean that they tell lies.

plead[pliːd]
v. 간청하다, 탄원하다; 변론하다, 변호하다
If you plead with someone to do something, you ask them in an intense, emotional way to do it.

keep it up
idiom 계속하다, 계속 해나가다
If you keep it up, you continue working or trying as hard as you have been in the past.

criminal[krímənl]
n. 범죄자, 범인
A criminal is a person who regularly commits crimes.

jail[dʒeil]
n. 교도소, 감옥
A jail is a place where criminals are kept in order to punish them, or where people waiting to be tried are kept.

assert[əsə́ːrt]
v. 주장하다, 단언하다
If someone asserts a fact or belief, they state it firmly.

junk[dʒʌŋk]
n. 쓸모 없는 물건, 쓰레기
Junk is old and used goods that have little value and that you do not want any more.

stomp[stamp]
v. 쿵쿵거리며 걷다, 발을 구르다
If you stomp somewhere, you walk there with very heavy steps, often because you are angry.

26

1분에 몇 단어를 읽는지 리딩 속도를 측정해보세요.

$$\frac{885 \text{ words}}{\text{reading time ( ) sec}} \times 60 = (\quad) \text{ WPM}$$

Build Your Vocabulary

holler
[hálər]

v. 고함지르다, 큰 소리로 부르다; n. 외침, 큰 소리
If you holler, you shout loudly.

liar^{복습}
[laiər]

n. 거짓말쟁이
If you say that someone is a liar, you mean that they tell lies.

grit
[grit]

v. 이를 갈다; 쓸리다, 삐걱삐걱 (소리 나게) 하다
If you grit your teeth, you press your upper and lower teeth tightly together, usually because you are angry about something.

elect^{복습}
[ilékt]

v. 선거하다, 선출하다
When people elect someone, they choose that person to represent them, by voting for them.

fool*
[fu:l]

v. 속이다, 기만하다; n. 바보
If someone fools you, they deceive or trick you.

timid*
[tímid]

a. 소심한, 자신이 없는 (timidly ad. 소심하게)
If you describe someone's attitudes or actions as timid, you are criticizing them for being too cautious or slow to act.

bulletin board
[búlətin bɔ́:rd]

n. 게시판
A bulletin board is a board which is usually attached to a wall in order to display notices giving information about something.

startle^{복습}
[sta:rtl]

v. 깜짝 놀라게 하다; 움찔하다; n. 깜짝 놀람 (startled a. 깜짝 놀란)
If something sudden and unexpected startles you, it surprises and frightens you slightly.

scare**
[skɛər]

v. 위협하다, 겁나게 하다
If something scares you, it frightens or worries you.

deep down

idiom 사실은, 본심은; 마음속으로는
Deep down refers to in reality rather than in apprearance.

quality**
[kwáləti]

n. 소질, 재능; 질, 품질; 성질, 특성
Someone's qualities are the good characteristics that they have which are part of their nature.

hire^{복습}
[haiər]

v. 고용하다; 빌리다, 빌려주다; n. 고용
If you hire someone, you employ them or pay them to do a particular job for you.

counsel^{복습}
[káunsəl]

v. 상담을 하다; n. 조언, 충고 (counselor n. 지도교사, 상담사)
If you counsel people, you give them advice about their problems.

permit***
[pərmít]

v. 허가하다, 허락하다 (permission n. 허락, 허가)
If they permit you to do something, they allow you to do it.

drastic
[drǽstik]

a. (치료 · 변화 등이) 격렬한, 과감한
If you have to take drastic action in order to solve a problem, you have to do something extreme and basic to solve it.

measure**
[méʒər]

n. 조치, 정책; v. 측정하다, 재다
When someone, usually a government or other authority, takes measures to do something, they carry out particular actions in order to achieve a particular result.

hall^{복습}
[hɔːl]

n. (건물 안의) 복도; (건물 입구 안쪽의) 현관
A hall in a building is a long passage with doors into rooms on both sides of it.

content*
[kəntént]

① n. (pl.) (어떤 것의) 속에 든 것들, 내용물; 목차
② a. (자기가 가진 것에) 만족하는; v. ~에 자족하다
If you are content with something, you are willing to accept it, rather than wanting something more or something better.

spill^{복습}
[spil]

v. 엎지르다, 흘리다; n. 엎지름, 유출
If the contents of a bag, box, or other container spill or are spilled, they come out of the container onto a surface.

ladder*
[lǽdər]

n. 사다리
A ladder is a piece of equipment used for climbing up something or down from something.

lie^{복습}
[lai]

① v. (lay-lain) 놓여 있다, 위치하다; 눕다, 누워 있다 ② v. 거짓말하다; n. 거짓말
If an object lies in a particular place, it is in a flat position in that place.

surround**
[səráund]

v. 둘러싸다, 에워싸다; n. 둘러싸는 것; 환경, 주위
If a person or thing is surrounded by something, that thing is situated all around them.

hardly***
[háːrdli]

ad. 거의 ~아니다, 전혀 ~않다
You use hardly to modify a statement when you want to emphasize that it is only a small amount or detail which makes it true, and that therefore it is best to consider the opposite statement as being true.

move in

idiom 이사를 들다; (위협적으로) 사방에서 접근하다
If you move in, you go to a new house and begin to live there

shrug^{복습}
[ʃrʌg]

v. (양 손바닥을 내보이면서 어깨를) 으쓱하다; n. 으쓱하기
If you shrug, you raise your shoulders to show that you are not interested in something or that you do not know or care about something.

grunt*
[grʌnt]

n. 툴툴거리는 소리; v. (사람이) 툴툴거리다; (돼지가) 꿀꿀거리다
A grunt is a low sound you make, especially because you are annoyed or not interested in something.

blond*
[bland]

a. 금발의
Blond hair is very light brown or light yellow.

remove[**]
[rimúːv]

v. 제거하다, 치우다; 옮기다, 이사하다
If you remove something from a place, you take it away.

hopeless[*]
[hóuplis]

a. 가망 없는, 절망적인 (hopelessly ad. 절망하여)
Someone or something thing that is hopeless is certain to fail or be unsuccessful.

mutter[*]
[mʌ́tər]

v. 중얼거리다, 불평하다; n. 중얼거림, 불평
If you mutter, you speak very quietly so that you cannot easily be heard, often because you are complaining about something.

tear[복습]
[tɛər]

① v. 부리나케 가다; 찢다, 찢어지다; n. 찢음 ② n. 눈물
If you tear somewhere, you move there very quickly, often in an uncontrolled or dangerous way.

mess[*]
[mes]

n. 엉망진창, 난잡함; v. 망쳐놓다, 방해하다 (messy a. 지저분한, 엉망인)
If you say that something is a mess or in a mess, you think that it is in an untidy state.

nod[**]
[nad]

v. 끄덕이다, 끄덕여 표시하다; n. (동의 · 인사 · 신호 · 명령의) 끄덕임
If you nod, you move your head downward and upward to show agreement, understanding, or approval.

horror[*]
[hɔ́ːrər]

n. 공포, 전율 (horror story n. 끔찍한 이야기)
Horror is a feeling of great shock, fear, and worry caused by something extremely unpleasant.

warn[***]
[wɔːrn]

v. 경고하다; ~에게 통지하다
If you warn someone about something such as a possible danger or problem, you tell them about it so that they are aware of it.

drop by

idiom 잠깐 들르다, 불시에 찾아가다
If you drop by, you pay a short, informal visit to someone, often without arranging this in advance.

interrupt[**]
[ìntərʌ́pt]

v. 방해하다, 가로막다, 저지하다
If you interrupt someone who is speaking, you say or do something that causes them to stop.

charming[*]
[ʧɑ́ːrmiŋ]

a. 매력 있는, 매력적인
If you say that something is charming, you mean that it is very pleasant or attractive.

delight[*]
[diláit]

v. 즐겁게 하다, 매우 기쁘게 하다; n. 기쁨, 즐거움 (delightful a. 유쾌한)
If you describe something or someone as delightful, you mean they are very pleasant.

1. What did Bradley's mother say at dinner about how
   Bradley was doing in school?
   A. She said he was doing very poorly.
   B. She said he was doing very well.
   C. She said he was the class president.
   D. She said he should go to military school.

2. How did Bradley react to Jeff offering to help with his
   homework?
   A. Bradley wanted Jeff to do his homework for him.
   B. Bradley said that Jeff could help him get a gold star.
   C. Bradley said that he was the smartest kid in class and could help
      Jeff instead.
   D. Bradley said that he was the smartest kid in class and didn't need
      help.

3. Why was Jeff going to see the counselor?
   A. He was in trouble for fighting other students.
   B. He was having trouble with his homework.
   C. He was new and needed to adjust to the new school.
   D. Everyone in school had to go see the counselor.

4. Why did Jeff go into the girls' bathroom?
   A. He was curious about how it looked.
   B. He was lost and went in by accident.
   C. He couldn't find the boys' bathroom.
   D. He thought that it was the boys' bathroom.

5. Who was in the bathroom when Jeff entered?
   A. A girl with red hair and freckles
   B. A girl with brown hair and freckles
   C. A girl with black hair and no freckles
   D. Nobody else

6. Who did Carla tell about the topics that students told her?
   A. She told the principal.
   B. She told their parents.
   C. She told their friends.
   D. She told nobody else.

7. Why did the girls come to Jeff and Bradley at lunch?
   A. They wanted to be friends with Jeff and Bradley.
   B. They wanted to invite Jeff and Bradley to a party.
   C. They wanted to know Jeff's name and why he was in the girls' bathroom.
   D. They wanted to know why Jeff was really being friends with Bradley.

1분에 몇 단어를 읽는지 리딩 속도를 측정해보세요.

$$\frac{331 \text{ words}}{\text{reading time (} \quad \text{) sec}} \times 60 = (\qquad) \text{ WPM}$$

Build Your Vocabulary

mash
[mæʃ]

v. 으깨다, 짓찧다, 짓이기다 (mashed potato n. 삶아 으깬 감자)
If you mash something, you crush it so that it forms a soft mass.

military**
[mílitèri]

n. 군대, 군인들; a. 군사의, 무력의 (military school n. 사관 학교)
The military are the armed forces of a country.

drizzle
[drizl]

v. 이슬비가 내리다; n. 이슬비, 가랑비
If it is drizzling, it is raining very lightly.

rubber**
[rʌ́bər]

a. 고무의; n. 고무 (rubber boots n. 고무장화)
Rubber things are made of a strong, waterproof, elastic substance made from the juice of a tropical tree or produced chemically.

stamp^{복습}
[stæmp]

v. (발을) 구르다, 짓밟다; (도장 · 스탬프 등을) 찍다; n. 우표, 인지; 도장
If you stamp or stamp your foot, you lift your foot and put it down very hard on the ground, for example because you are angry.

puddle
[pʌdl]

n. 웅덩이; 뒤범벅; v. 흙탕물을 휘젓다
A puddle is a small, shallow pool of liquid that has spread on the ground.

splash*
[splæʃ]

n. 튀기기; 첨벙 튀기는 소리; v. (물 · 흙탕 등) 튀기다, 첨벙거리다
A splash of a liquid is a small quantity of it that falls on something or is added to something.

overhang*
[òuvərhǽŋ]

n. (지붕 · 발코니 등의) 돌출부; v. (~위로) 돌출하다
An overhang is the part of something that sticks out over and above something else.

stare^{복습}
[stɛər]

v. 응시하다, 뚫어지게 보다
If you stare at someone or something, you look at them for a long time.

convince*
[kənvíns]

v. 설득하다, 확신시키다, 납득시키다
If someone or something convinces you of something, they make you believe that it is true or that it exists.

greet**
[griːt]

v. 인사하다; 환영하다, 맞이하다
When you greet someone, you say 'Hello' or shake hands with them.

offer***
[ɔ́ːfər]

v. 제의하다, 제안하다; 제공하다; n. 제공
If you offer something to someone, you ask them if they would like to have it or use it.

stuff^{복습}
[stʌf]

n. 것(들), 물건, 물질; v. 채워 넣다, 속을 채우다
You can use stuff to refer to things such as a substance, a collection of things, events, or ideas in a general way without mentioning the thing itself by name.

modest**
[mádist]

a. 겸손한; 신중한; 적당한 (modestly ad. 겸손하게, 조심성 있게)
If you say that someone is modest, you approve of them because they do not talk much about their abilities or achievements.

outer space
[áutər speis]

n. (대기권 외) 우주 공간
Outer space is the area outside the earth's atmosphere where the other planets and stars are situated.

side by side

idiom 나란히
If two people or things are side by side, they are next to each other.

necessarily*
[nesəsárəli]

ad. 어쩔 수 없이, 필연적으로
If you say that something is not necessarily the case, you mean that it may not be the case or is not always the case.

1분에 몇 단어를 읽는지 리딩 속도를 측정해보세요.

$$\frac{491 \text{ words}}{\text{reading time ( ) sec}} \times 60 = (\quad) \text{ WPM}$$

Build Your Vocabulary

hopeless^{복습}
[hóuplis]

a. 가망 없는, 절망적인 (hopelessly ad. 절망하여)
Someone or something thing that is hopeless is certain to fail or be unsuccessful.

clutch*
[klʌʧ]

v. 꽉 잡다, 붙들다, 부여잡다; n. 움켜쥠
If you clutch at something or clutch something, you hold it tightly, usually because you are afraid or anxious.

corridor*
[kɔ́:ridər]

n. 복도
A corridor is a long passage in a building or train, with doors and rooms on one or both sides.

adjust**
[ədʒʌ́st]

v. 적응하다, 적합시키다; (옷매무새 등을) 바로 하다; 조절하다, 조정하다
When you adjust to a new situation, you get used to it by changing your behavior or your ideas.

slippery*
[slípəri]

a. 미끄러운, 미끈거리는
Something that is slippery is smooth, wet, or oily and is therefore difficult to walk on or to hold.

recess^{복습}
[rí:ses]

n. (학교의) 쉬는 시간; 휴회
A recess is a short period of time when you have a rest or a change from what you are doing, especially if you are working or if you are in a boring or unpleasant situation.

track**
[træk]

v. 발자국을 내다, (진흙 등을) 발에 묻혀들이다; ~의 뒤를 쫓다; n. 지나간 자취
If you track something somewhere, you make a train of footprints with it around there.

stack*
[stæk]

n. 더미; 많음, 다량; v. 쌓다, 쌓아올리다
A stack of things is a pile of them.

tremble*
[trembl]

v. 떨다, 떨리다
If you tremble, you shake slightly because you are frightened or cold.

wing**
[wiŋ]

n. (건물 본관 한쪽으로 돌출되게 지은) 동(棟), 부속 건물; 날개; v. 날아가다
A wing of a building is a part of it which sticks out from the main part.

count***
[kaunt]

v. 수를 세다, 계산하다; 중요하다; (정식으로) 인정되다; n. 셈, 계산
When you count, you say all the numbers one after another up to a particular number.

freckle
[frekl]

n. 주근깨, 반점, 기미 (freckled a. 주근깨가 있는)
Freckles are small light brown spots on someone's skin, especially on their face.

34

sink*
[siŋk]

n. 세면대; (부엌의) 싱크대, 개수대; v. 가라앉다, 빠지다
A sink is a large bowl, usually with taps for hot and cold water, for washing your hands and face.

utter*
[ʌ́tər]

v. (신음 소리 · 한숨 등을) 내다, 지르다; 말하다, 발언하다
If someone utters sounds or words, they say them.

yell복습
[jel]

v. 소리치다, 고함치다; n. 고함소리, 부르짖음
If you yell, you shout loudly, usually because you are excited, angry, or in pain.

freeze**
[fri:z]

v. (froze–frozen) 얼다, 얼리다; n. (임금 · 가격 등의) 동결
If someone who is moving freezes, they suddenly stop and become completely still and quiet.

dash*
[dæʃ]

v. 돌진하다; 내던지다; n. 돌격
If you dash somewhere, you run or go there quickly and suddenly.

race복습
[reis]

① v. 질주하다, 달리다; 경주하다; n. 경주 ② n. 인종, 민족
If you race somewhere, you go there as quickly as possible.

slip*
[slip]

v. 미끄러지다; 살짝 나오다, 살짝 들어가다; n. (작은 종이) 조각, 쪽지
If you slip, you accidentally slide and lose your balance.

flop
[flap]

v. 펄썩[털썩] 쓰러지다; 퍼덕거리다; n. 펄썩 떨어짐
If something flops onto something else, it falls there heavily or untidily.

groan*
[groun]

v. 신음하다, 끙끙거리다; n. 신음, 끙끙거리는 소리
If you groan, you make a long, low sound because you are in pain, or because you are upset or unhappy about something.

frantic*
[frǽntik]

a. 극도로 흥분한, 광란의 (frantically ad. 미친 듯이)
If you are frantic, you are behaving in a wild and uncontrolled way because you are frightened or worried.

opposite**
[ápəzit]

a. 반대편의, 맞은편의; 정반대의; n. 정반대의 일; ad. 정반대의 위치에
If one thing is opposite another, it is on the other side of a space from it.

spot**
[spat]

v. 발견하다, 분별하다; n. 장소, 지점; 반점, 얼룩
If you spot something or someone, you notice them.

round**
[raund]

v. (모퉁이 · 커브 등을) 돌다; 둥글게 만들다; a. 둥근, 동그란, 원형의
If you round a place or obstacle, you move in a curve past the edge or corner of it.

storage*
[stɔ́:ridʒ]

n. 저장(고), 창고
If you refer to the storage of something, you mean that it is kept in a special place until it is needed.

clutter
[klʌ́tər]

v. (장소를) 어지르다; 혼란케 하다; n. 난장판, 어지러움, 혼란
If things or people clutter a place, they fill it in an untidy way.

duck
[dʌk]

① v. 피하다, 머리를 홱 숙이다 ② n. 오리
If you duck, you move your head or the top half of your body quickly downward to avoid something that might hit you, or to avoid being seen.

spin^{**}
[spin]

v. (spun–spun) 돌다, 맴돌리다; 오래[질질] 끌다; n. 회전
If something spins or if you spin it, it turns quickly around a central point.

ladder^{복습}
[lǽdər]

n. 사다리
A ladder is a piece of equipment used for climbing up something or down from something.

Check Your Reading Speed

1분에 몇 단어를 읽는지 리딩 속도를 측정해보세요.

$$\frac{827 \text{ words}}{\text{reading time } (\quad) \text{ sec}} \times 60 = (\quad) \text{ WPM}$$

Build Your Vocabulary

counsel^{복습}
[káunsəl]

v. 상담을 하다; n. 조언, 충고 (counselor n. 지도교사, 상담사)
If you counsel people, you give them advice about their problems.

echo[*]
[ékou]

v. 울려 퍼지다, 메아리치다; (남의 말·의견을) 그대로 되풀이하다; n. 메아리
If a sound echoes, it is reflected off a surface and can be heard again after the original sound has stopped.

scary
[skéəri]

a. 무서운, 두려운
Something that is scary is rather frightening.

frown^{복습}
[fraun]

v. 얼굴을 찡그리다, 눈살을 찌푸리다; n. 찌푸린 얼굴
When someone frowns, their eyebrows become drawn together, because they are annoyed or puzzled.

sort of

idiom 다소, 얼마간, 말하자면
You use sort of when you want to say that your description of something is not very accurate.

spit^{복습}
[spit]

v. (침 등을) 뱉다; 내뱉듯이 말하다; n. 침
If someone spits, they force an amount of liquid out of their mouth, often to show hatred or contemp.

break even

idiom 득실이 없다, 수지가 맞아 떨어지다
When a company or a person running a business breaks even, they make neither a profit nor a loss.

dozen^{**}
[dʌzn]

n. 12개; 수십, 다수
If you have a dozen things, you have twelve of them.

hang around

idiom (~에서) 서성거리다
If you hang around, you spend time somewhere, without doing very much.

principal[*]
[prínsəpəl]

n. 장(長), 교장; a. 주요한, 제1의
The principal of a school or a college, is the person in charge of the school or college.

grimace
[gríməs]

v. 얼굴을 찡그리다; n. 얼굴을 찡그림
If you grimace, you twist your face in an ugly way because you are annoyed, disgusted, or in pain.

accidental^{복습}
[æksədéntl]

a. 우연한; 부수적인 (accidentally ad. 우연히)
An accidental event happens by chance or as the result of an accident, and is not deliberately intended.

1분에 몇 단어를 읽는지 리딩 속도를 측정해보세요.

$$\frac{924 \text{ words}}{\text{reading time (\quad) sec}} \times 60 = (\qquad) \text{ WPM}$$

Build Your Vocabulary

geography**
[dʒiágrəfi]

n. 지리학; 지형, 지세
Geography is the study of the countries of the world and of such things as the land, seas, climate, towns, and population.

stick복습
[stik]

① v. (stuck–stuck) 내밀다; 찔러 넣다, 찌르다; 붙이다, 달라붙다
② n. 막대기, 지팡이
If something is sticking out from a surface or object, it extends up or away from it.

scissors복습
[sízərz]

n. 가위
Scissors are a small cutting tool with two sharp blades that are screwed together.

edge**
[edʒ]

n. 가장자리, 변두리, 끝; v. 조금씩[살살] 움직이다; 테두리를 두르다
The edge of something is the place or line where it stops, or the part of it that is furthest from the middle.

horrible**
[hɔ́:rəbl]

a. 끔찍한, 소름 끼치게 싫은; 무서운
You can call something horrible when it causes you to feel great shock, fear, and disgust.

tape복습
[teip]

v. (접착) 테이프로 붙이다; 녹음하다, 녹화하다;
n. (소리 · 영상을 기록하는) 테이프; (접착용) 테이프 (taper n. 테이프 붙이는 사람)
If you tape one thing to another, you attach it using sticky strip of plastic.

mess복습
[mes]

n. 엉망진창, 난잡함; v. 망쳐놓다, 방해하다 (messy a. 지저분한, 엉망인)
If you say that something is a mess or in a mess, you think that it is in an untidy state.

twist복습
[twist]

v. 비틀다, 돌리다, 꼬다; n. 뒤틀림; 엉킴
If you twist something, you turn it to make a spiral shape, for example by turning the two ends of it in opposite directions.

hall복습
[hɔ:l]

n. (건물 안의) 복도; (건물 입구 안쪽의) 현관
A hall in a building is a long passage with doors into rooms on both sides of it.

hook**
[huk]

n. 갈고리, 훅, 걸쇠; v. 갈고리로 걸다
A hook is a bent piece of metal or plastic that is used for catching or holding things, or for hanging things up.

shove*
[ʃʌv]

v. (아무렇게나) 밀어넣다; 밀치다, 떠밀다; n. 밀치기
If you shove something somewhere, you push it there quickly and carelessly.

sack*
[sæk]

n. (쇼핑 물건을 담는 크고 튼튼한 종이) 봉지; 부대, 자루; v. 자루에 넣다
Sacks are used to carry or store things such as vegetables or coal.

auditorium
[ɔ̀:ditɔ́:riəm]

n. 강당, 회관; 청중석, 관객석
An auditorium is a large room, hall, or building which is used for events such as meetings and concerts.

sort of^{복습}

idiom 다소, 얼마간, 말하자면
You use sort of when you want to say that your description of something is not very accurate.

steam**
[sti:m]

v. 증기가 발생하다; (식품 등을) 찌다; n. 증기 (steamy a. 습한)
If something steams, it gives off hot mist.

ignore**
[ignɔ́:r]

v. 무시하다, 모르는 체하다
If you ignore someone or something, you pay no attention to them.

tiptoe
[típtòu]

n. 발끝; v. 발끝으로 걷다, 발돋움하다
If you do something on tiptoe or on tiptoes, you do it standing or walking on the front part of your foot, without putting your heels on the ground.

locate*
[lóukeit]

v. (물건의 위치 등을) 알아내다; (어떤 장소에) 위치하다, 두다, 놓다
If you locate something or someone, you find out where they are.

peanut*
[pí:nʌt]

n. 땅콩 (peanut butter n. 땅콩 버터)
Peanuts are small nuts that grow under the ground. Peanuts are often eaten as a snack, especially roasted and salted.

tuna*
[tjú:nə]

n. 참치 (tuna fish n. 참치의 살코기)
Tuna or tuna fish are large fish that live in warm seas and are caught for food.

swallow**
[swálou]

v. 삼키다, 목구멍으로 넘기다; (초조해서) 마른침을 삼키다
If you swallow something, you cause it to go from your mouth down into your stomach.

chop*
[tʃap]

v. 자르다, 잘게 썰다; n. 절단; 잘라낸 조각
If you chop something, you cut it into pieces with strong downward movements of a knife or an ax.

suck**
[sʌk]

v. 빨다, 흡수하다; n. 빨아들임
If something sucks a liquid, gas, or object in a particular direction, it draws the object there with a powerful force.

straw*
[strɔ:]

n. 빨대; 지푸라기, 짚
A straw is a thin tube of paper or plastic, which you use to suck a drink into your mouth.

gurgle
[gə:rgl]

v. (물이 좁은 공간을 빠르게 흐를 때 나는) 꼴꼴 소리 나다; n. 꼴깍 하는 소리
If water is gurgling, it is making the sound that it makes when it flows quickly and unevenly through a narrow space.

freckle^{복습}
[frekl]

n. 주근깨, 반점, 기미 (freckled a. 주근깨가 있는)
Freckles are small light brown spots on someone's skin, especially on their face.

whisper*
[hwíspər]

v. 속삭이다
When you whisper, you say something very quietly.

throw up^{복습}

idiom ~을 토하다, 게우다
When someone throws up, they bring food they have eaten back out of mouth.

shrug^{복습}
[ʃrʌg]

v. (양 손바닥을 내보이면서 어깨를) 으쓱하다; n. 으쓱하기
If you shrug, you raise your shoulders to show that you are not interested in something or that you do not know or care about something.

bite**
[bait]

v. (bit–bit) 물다, 물어뜯다; n. 물기; 한 입(의 분량)
If you bite into something, you use your teeth to cut into it, for example in order to eat it or break it.

ferocious
[fəróuʃəs]

a. 흉포한, 맹렬한 (ferociously ad. 사납게)
A ferocious animal, person, or action is very fierce and violent.

blush*
[blʌʃ]

v. 얼굴을 붉히다, (얼굴이) 빨개지다; n. 얼굴을 붉힘, 홍조
When you blush, your face becomes redder than usual because you are ashamed or embarrassed.

skinny
[skíni]

a. 바싹 여윈, 깡마른
A skinny person is extremely thin, often in a way that you find unattractive.

plead^{복습}
[pliːd]

v. 간청하다, 탄원하다; 변론하다, 변호하다
If you plead with someone to do something, you ask them in an intense, emotional way to do it.

giggle^{복습}
[gigl]

v. 낄낄 웃다; n. 낄낄 웃음
If someone giggles, they laugh in a childlike way, because they are amused, nervous, or embarrassed.

rescue^{복습}
[réskjuː]

n. 구출, 구원; v. 구조하다, 구출하다
Rescue is help which gets someone out of a dangerous or unpleasant situation.

punch^{복습}
[pʌntʃ]

v. 주먹으로 치다, 때리다; n. 주먹으로 한 대 침, 펀치
If you punch someone or something, you hit them hard with your fist.

fist*
[fist]

n. (쥔) 주먹
Your hand is referred to as your fist when you have bent your fingers in toward the palm in order to hit someone, to make an angry gesture, or to hold something.

back away

idiom (~에서) 뒷걸음질치다, (~을) 피하다
If you back away, you move backward away from someone or something frightening or unpleasant.

screech*
[skriːtʃ]

v. 비명을 지르다, 꽥 하는 소리를 내다; n. 귀에 거슬리는 날카로운 소리
When you screech something, you shout it in a loud, unpleasant, high-pitched voice.

amaze^{복습}
[əméiz]

v. 깜짝 놀라게 하다 (amazed a. 깜짝 놀란)
If something amazes you, it surprises you very much.

40

elbow^{**}
[élbou]

n. 팔꿈치; v. 팔꿈치로 쿡 찌르다
Your elbow is the part of your arm where the upper and lower halves
of the arm are joined.

declare^{***}
[dikléər]

v. 선언하다; 단언하다
If you declare something, you state officially and formally that it exists
or is the case.

chapters 9 to 12

1. Where did Bradley say he was going when he met the teacher in the hall?
   A. He said he was going to the nurse's office to get medicine.
   B. He said he was going to the counselor's office to talk.
   C. He said he was going to the library to get a book.
   D. He said he was going to the cafeteria to get lunch.

2. What did Carla not believe in that Bradley thought was crazy?
   A. Carla didn't believe in drinking milk.
   B. Carla didn't believe in accidents.
   C. Carla didn't believe in geography.
   D. Carla didn't believe in messes.

3. What did Bradley do with the drawing he made?
   A. He gave it to Carla for free.
   B. He gave it to Carla for a dollar.
   C. He hung it up on the wall.
   D. He crumpled it up and threw it away.

4. Which of the following is NOT true about Bradley and the girls' bathroom?

   A. He wanted to go inside a girls' bathroom.

   B. He had never been inside a girls' bathroom.

   C. He hoped Jeff would take him inside one.

   D. He imagined that it would look like a boys' bathroom.

5. Why did Jeff say that it wasn't a good time to go inside the girls' bathroom after school?

   A. Because there wouldn't be girls.

   B. Because the doors were locked.

   C. Because there would be teachers.

   D. Because they should go during lunch.

6. How did Jeff react when someone said hello to him?

   A. He didn't say anything.

   B. He smiled at them.

   C. He always said hello back.

   D. He always said you're welcome.

7. Why did Colleen go to see Carla?

   A. She wanted to ask for a form for her parents to sign.

   B. She wanted advice on inviting Jeff to her birthday party.

   C. She wanted advice to help Bradley make more friends.

   D. She wanted to know secrets about Lori.

1분에 몇 단어를 읽는지 리딩 속도를 측정해보세요.

$$\frac{1{,}314 \text{ words}}{\text{reading time ( ) sec}} \times 60 = (\quad) \text{ WPM}$$

Build Your Vocabulary

detour
[díːtuər]

n. 우회, 우회로(路); v. 우회하다, 에움길로 가다
If you make a detour on a journey, you go by a route which is not the shortest way, because you want to avoid something such as a traffic jam.

allow***
[əláu]

v. 허락하다, ~하게 두다; 인정하다
If someone is allowed to do something, it is all right for them to do it and they will not get into trouble.

check out

idiom (책 등을) 빌리다, 대출하다
If you check something out, you borrow it such as a book or a video from a library.

announce^{복습}
[ənáuns]

v. 발표하다, 알리다
If you announce something, you tell people about it publicly or officially.

look forward to

idiom ~을 고대하다
To look forward to means to feel excited about something that is going to happen because you expect to enjoy it.

expect***
[ikspékt]

v. 예상하다, 기대하다
If you expect something to happen, you believe that it will happen.

hag
[hæg]

n. (심술궂은) 추한 노파
If someone refers to a woman as a hag, they mean that she is ugly, old, and unpleasant.

blond^{복습}
[bland]

a. 금발의
Blond hair is very light brown or light yellow.

squiggle
[skwigl]

n. 구불구불한 선; v. 휘갈겨 쓰다 (squiggly ad. 구불구불한)
A squiggle is a line that bends and curls in an irregular way.

scribble^{복습}
[skribl]

v. 낙서하다; 갈겨쓰다, 휘갈기다; n. 낙서
To scribble means to make meaningless marks or rough drawings using a pencil or pen.

stare^{복습}
[stɛər]

v. 응시하다, 뚫어지게 보다
If you stare at someone or something, you look at them for a long time.

on purpose

idiom 고의로, 일부로
If you do something on purpose, you do it intentionally.

44

appreciate[**] [əprí:ʃièit]
v. 고맙게 생각하다; 평가하다, 감상하다
If you appreciate something that someone has done for you or is going to do for you, you are grateful for it.

by accident
idiom 우연히
If you say that something happens by accident, you mean that it has not been planned.

spill[복습] [spil]
v. 엎지르다, 흘리다; n. 엎지름, 유출
If a liquid spills or if you spill it, it accidentally flows over the edge of a container.

trick[**] [trik]
v. 속이다, 속임수를 쓰다; n. 속임수; 비결, 요령; 묘기, 재주
If someone tricks you, they deceive you, often in order to make you do something.

glance[복습] [glæns]
v. 흘긋 보다, 잠깐 보다; n. 흘긋 봄
If you glance at something or someone, you look at them very quickly and then look away again immediately.

object[***] [ɔ́bdʒikt]
n. 물건, 물체; 목적, 목표; v. 반대하다, 이의를 주장하다
An object is anything that has a fixed shape or form that you can touch or see, and that is not alive.

admit[복습] [ædmít]
v. 인정하다
If you admit that something bad, unpleasant, or embarrassing is true, you agree, often unwillingly, that it is true.

depress[*] [diprés]
v. 우울하게 하다, 낙담시키다 (depressing a. 우울한)
If someone or something depresses you, they make you feel sad and disappointed.

remind[복습] [rimáind]
v. 생각나게 하다, 상기시키다, 일깨우다
If someone reminds you of a fact or event that you already know about, they say something which makes you think about it.

declare[복습] [dikléər]
v. 선언하다; 단언하다
If you declare that something is true, you say that it is true in a firm, deliberate way.

squirm [skwə:rm]
v. 몸부림치다, (벌레처럼) 꿈틀거리다; 우물쭈물하다
If you squirm, you move your body from side to side, usually because you are nervous or uncomfortable.

geography[복습] [dʒiágrəfi]
n. 지리학; 지형, 지세
Geography is the study of the countries of the world and of such things as the land, seas, climate, towns, and population.

mouse[**] [maus]
n. (pl. mice) [동물] 쥐, 생쥐
A mouse is a small furry animal with a long tail.

trunk[*] [trʌŋk]
n. 코끼리 코; 여행 가방; (나무의) 줄기, 몸뚱이
An elephant's trunk is its very long nose that it uses to lift food and water to its mouth.

stuck[**] [stʌk]
a. 꽉 끼인, 움직일 수 없는, 곤경에 빠진; v. STICK의 과거·과거분사
If something is stuck in a particular position, it is fixed tightly in this position and is unable to move.

breathe
[briːð]

v. 호흡하다, 숨을 쉬다
When people or animals breathe, they take air into their lungs and let it out again.

share^{복습}
[ʃɛər]

v. 공유하다; 분배하다; n. 몫, 분담
If you share something with another person, you both have it, use it, or occupy it.

fountain[*]
[fáuntən]

n. 분수; 샘
A fountain is an ornamental feature in a pool or lake which consists of a long narrow stream of water that is forced up into the air.

in time

idiom 제시간에, 늦지 않고, 때맞추어
If you do something in time, it means that you are not late to do it.

mood
[muːd]

n. 기분, 심정; 분위기
If you say that you are in the mood for something, you mean that you want to do it or have it.

assure[*]
[əʃúər]

v. 단언하다, 확신하다, 보증하다
If you assure someone that something is true or will happen, you tell them that it is definitely true or will definitely happen, often in order to make them less worried.

bare[*]
[bɛər]

a. 발가벗은; 아무것도 안 덮인; v. (신체의 일부를) 드러내다
(with bare hands idiom 맨손으로)
If someone does something with their bare hands, they do it without using any weapons or tools.

feed^{복습}
[fiːd]

v. (fed-fed) 먹이를 주다, 음식을 먹이다; 공급하다
If you feed a person or animal, you give them food to eat and sometimes actually put it in their mouths.

meaty
[míːti]

a. 고기 같은, 고기가 많은; 살찐
Food that is meaty contains a lot of meat.

right away

idiom 곧바로, 즉시
If you do something right away, you do it immediately.

session[*]
[séʃən]

n. (특정한 활동을 위한) 시간, 기간; 회의, 회기
A session of a particular activity is a period of that activity.

construct[*]
[kənstrʌ́kt]

v. 조립하다; 구성하다; n. 구조물 (construction paper n. 판지, 마분지)
If you construct something such as a building, road, or machine, you build it or make it.

lean^{복습}
[liːn]

v. 기울다, 기울이다, (몸을) 숙이다; ~에 기대다; ~을 ~에 기대 놓다
When you lean in a particular direction, you bend your body in that direction.

barber[*]
[báːrbər]

n. 이발사
A barber is a man whose job is cutting men's hair.

curly[*]
[kə́ːrli]

a. 곱슬곱슬한
Curly hair is full of curls.

worth[**]
[wəːrθ]

a. ~의 가치가 있는; n. 가치, 값어치
If something is worth a particular amount of money, it can be sold for that amount or is considered to have that value.

back away[복습]

idiom (~에서) 뒷걸음질치다, (~을) 피하다
If you back away, you move backward away from someone or something frightening or unpleasant.

poisonous[*]
[pɔ́izənəs]

a. 유독한, 독성의; 유해한
Something that is poisonous will kill you or make you ill if you swallow or absorb it.

wastepaper
[wéistpèipər]

n. 휴지, 폐지 (wastepaper basket n. 휴지통)
A wastepaper basket is a container for rubbish, especially paper, which is usually placed on the floor in the corner of a room or next to a desk.

crumple
[krʌmpl]

v. 구기다, 쭈글쭈글하게 하다; 구겨지다; n. 주름
If you crumple something such as paper or cloth, or if it crumples, it is squashed and becomes full of untidy creases and folds.

1분에 몇 단어를 읽는지 리딩 속도를 측정해보세요.

$$\frac{563 \text{ words}}{\text{reading time } (\quad) \text{ sec}} \times 60 = (\qquad) \text{ WPM}$$

Build Your Vocabulary

row^{복습}
[rou]

① n. 열, 줄 ② v. 노를 젓다, 배를 젓다; n. 노 젓기
A row of things or people is a number of them arranged in a line.

counsel^{복습}
[káunsəl]

v. 상담을 하다; n. 조언, 충고 (counselor n. 지도교사, 상담사)
If you counsel people, you give them advice about their problems.

scare^{복습}
[skɛər]

v. 위협하다, 겁나게 하다
If something scares you, it frightens or worries you.

alike***
[əláik]

a. (아주) 비슷한
If two or more things are alike, they are similar in some way.

sneak*
[sni:k]

v. 살금살금 가다, 몰래 가다
If you sneak somewhere, you go there very quietly on foot, trying to avoid being seen or heard.

courage***
[kə́:ridʒ]

n. 용기, 담력
Courage is the quality shown by someone who decides to do something difficult or dangerous, even though they may be afraid.

peek
[pi:k]

v. 살짝 들여다보다, 엿보다; n. 엿봄
If you peek at something or someone, you have a quick look at them.

be dying to

idiom ~하고 싶어 안달나다
If someone is dying to do something, they want to do it very much.

carpet*
[ká:rpit]

v. 양탄자를 깔다, 양탄자로 뒤덮다; n. 카펫, 양탄자
If a floor or a room is carpeted, a carpet is laid on the floor.

wallpaper
[wɔ́:lpéipər]

n. 벽지; v. (벽·천장 등에) 벽지를 바르다
Wallpaper is thick colored or patterned paper that is used for covering and decorating the walls of rooms.

toilet*
[tɔ́ilit]

n. 변기; 화장실
A toilet is a large bowl with a seat, or a platform with a hole, which is connected to a water system and which you use when you want to get rid of urine or feces from your body.

fountain^{복습}
[fáuntən]

n. 분수; 샘
A fountain is an ornamental feature in a pool or lake which consists of a long narrow stream of water that is forced up into the air.

sidewalk*
[sáidwɔ:k]

n. (포장한) 보도, 인도
A sidewalk is a path with a hard surface by the side of a road.

weird*
[wiərd]

a. 이상한, 기묘한; 수상한
If you describe something or someone as weird, you mean that they are strange.

make a face 복습

idiom 얼굴을 찌푸리다
If you make a face, you twist your face to indicate a certain mental or emotional state.

nod 복습
[nad]

v. 끄덕이다, 끄덕여 표시하다; n. (동의 · 인사 · 신호 · 명령의) 끄덕임
If you nod, you move your head downward and upward to show agreement, understanding, or approval.

distort 복습
[distɔ́:rt]

v. (얼굴 등을) 찡그리다, 찌푸리다; 비틀다; 왜곡하다
(distorted a. 찌그러진, 일그러진)
If someone's face or body distorts or is distorted, it moves into an unnatural and unattractive shape or position.

recess 복습
[ríːses]

n. (학교의) 쉬는 시간; 휴회
A recess is a short period of time when you have a rest or a change from what you are doing, especially if you are working or if you are in a boring or unpleasant situation.

blush 복습
[blʌʃ]

v. 얼굴을 붉히다, (얼굴이) 빨개지다; n. 얼굴을 붉힘, 홍조
When you blush, your face becomes redder than usual because you are ashamed or embarrassed.

mutter* 복습
[mʌ́tər]

v. 중얼거리다, 불평하다; n. 중얼거림, 불평
If you mutter, you speak very quietly so that you cannot easily be heard, often because you are complaining about something.

automatic*
[ɔ̀ːtəmǽtik]

a. 무의식적인, 반사적인; (기계가) 자동의
(automatically ad. 무의식적으로, 자동적으로)
An automatic action is one that you do without thinking about it.

reflex
[ríːfleks]

n. 반사 작용, 반사 운동; a. 반사적인
A reflex or a reflex action is something that you do automatically and without thinking, as a habit or as a reaction to something.

tap*
[tæp]

① v. 가볍게 두드리다; n. 가볍게 두드리기 ② n. 주둥이, (수도 등의) 꼭지
If you tap something, you hit it with a quick light blow or a series of quick light blows.

make sense

idiom 뜻이 통하다, 도리에 맞다
If something makes sense, it has a meaning that you can easily understand.

1분에 몇 단어를 읽는지 리딩 속도를 측정해보세요.

$$\frac{717 \text{ words}}{\text{reading time (\quad) sec}} \times 60 = (\qquad) \text{ WPM}$$

Build Your Vocabulary

digest*
[didʒést]
v. (음식을) 소화하다; (지식 등을) 잘 이해하다, 터득하다
When food digests or when you digest it, it passes through your body to your stomach.

thrill*
[θril]
v. 흥분시키다; 오싹하다; n. 전율, 오싹함 (thrilled a. 신이 난)
If something thrills you, or if you thrill at it, it gives you a feeling of great pleasure and excitement.

earn***
[əːrn]
v. 획득하다, 얻다; (돈을) 벌다
If you earn something such as praise, you get it because you deserve it.

hesitate***
[hézətèit]
v. 주저하다, 머뭇거리다, 망설이다
If you hesitate, you do not speak or act for a short time, usually because you are uncertain, embarrassed, or worried about what you are going to say or do.

bold*
[bould]
a. 대담한, 과감한; (선 등이) 굵은 (boldly ad. 대담하게)
Someone who is bold is not afraid to do things which involve risk or danger.

state***
[steit]
v. 분명히 말하다, 확언하다; n. 상태, 형편; 국가, 나라
If you state something, you say or write it in a formal or definite way.

assert복습
[əsə́ːrt]
v. 주장하다, 단언하다
If someone asserts a fact or belief, they state it firmly.

weird복습
[wiərd]
a. 이상한, 기묘한; 수상한
If you describe something or someone as weird, you mean that they are strange.

trick복습
[trik]
n. 속임수; 비결, 요령; 묘기, 재주; v. 속이다, 속임수를 쓰다
A trick is an action that is intended to deceive someone.

bounce*
[bauns]
v. 튀다, 튀게 하다; 급히 움직이다, 뛰어다니다; n. 튐, 바운드
When an object such as a ball bounces or when you bounce it, it moves upward from a surface or away from it immediately after hitting it.

court**
[kɔːrt]
n. (테니스 · 배구 등의) 코트; 뜰, 안마당; 법정, 법원
A court is an area in which you play a game such as tennis, basketball, badminton, or squash.

grab복습
[græb]
v. 부여잡다, 움켜쥐다; n. 부여잡기
If you grab something, you take it or pick it up suddenly and roughly.

50

urge^{복습}
[əːrdʒ]

v. 촉구하다, 충고히다, 재촉하다; n. (강한) 충동
If you urge someone to do something, you try hard to persuade them to do it.

all the way

idiom 완전히; 내내
You can use all the way to emphasize that your remark applies to every part of a situation, activity, or period of time.

roof**
[ruːf]

n. 지붕
The roof of a building is the covering on top of it that protects the people and things inside from the weather.

whisper^{복습}
[hwíspər]

v. 속삭이다
When you whisper, you say something very quietly.

shrug^{복습}
[ʃrʌg]

v. (양 손바닥을 내보이면서 어깨를) 으쓱하다; n. 으쓱하기
If you shrug, you raise your shoulders to show that you are not interested in something or that you do not know or care about something.

beat**
[biːt]

v. 치다, 두드리다; 패배시키다, 이기다; (심장이) 고동치다; n. [음악] 박자, 고동
If you beat someone or something, you hit them very hard.

fed up

a. 지긋지긋한, 신물이 난
If you are fed up, you are unhappy, bored, or tired of something, especially something that you have been experiencing for a long time.

manure
[mənjúər]

n. 거름, 비료; v. ~에 비료를 주다, 땅을 갈다
Manure is animal feces, sometimes mixed with chemicals, that is spread on the ground in order to make plants grow healthy and strong.

twist^{복습}
[twist]

v. 비틀다, 돌리다, 꼬다; n. 뒤틀림; 엉킴
If you twist something, especially a part of your body, or if it twists, it moves into an unusual, uncomfortable, or bent position, for example because of being hit or pushed, or because you are upset.

anguish*
[ǽŋgwiʃ]

n. 괴로움, 고뇌, 번민; v. 괴로워하다, 괴롭히다
Anguish is great mental suffering or physical pain.

stuff^{복습}
[stʌf]

n. 것(들), 물건, 물질; v. 채워 넣다, 속을 채우다
You can use stuff to refer to things such as a substance, a collection of things, events, or ideas in a general way without mentioning the thing itself by name.

Check Your Reading Speed

1분에 몇 단어를 읽는지 리딩 속도를 측정해보세요.

$$\frac{379 \text{ words}}{\text{reading time (} \qquad \text{) sec}} \times 60 = (\qquad) \text{ WPM}$$

Build Your Vocabulary

period^{**}
[píːəriəd]

n. (학교의 일과를 나눠 놓은) 시간; 기간, 시기
At a school or college, a period is one of the parts that the day is divided into during which lessons or other activities take place.

knock^{복습}
[nak]

v. (문을) 두드리다, 노크하다; 치다, 부수다; n. 노크; 타격
If you knock on something such as a door or window, you hit it, usually several times, to attract someone's attention.

timid^{복습}
[tímid]

a. 소심한, 자신이 없는 (timidly ad. 소심하게)
If you describe someone's attitudes or actions as timid, you are criticizing them for being too cautious or slow to act.

prefer^{**}
[prifɔ́ːr]

v. ~을 좋아하다, 차라리 ~을 택하다
If you prefer someone or something, you like that person or thing better than another, and so you are more likely to choose them if there is a choice.

horrible^{복습}
[hɔ́ːrəbl]

a. 끔찍한, 소름 끼치게 싫은; 무서운
If you describe something or someone as horrible, you do not like them at all.

rotten[*]
[ratn]

a. 형편없는, 끔찍한; 썩은, 부패한
If you describe someone as rotten, you are insulting them or criticizing them because you think that they are very unpleasant or unkind.

exclaim^{복습}
[ikskléim]

v. 외치다, 소리치다
If you exclaim, you say or shout something suddenly because of surprise, fear and pleasure.

allow^{복습}
[əláu]

v. 허락하다, ~하게 두다; 인정하다
If someone is allowed to do something, it is all right for them to do it and they will not get into trouble.

permit^{복습}
[pərmít]

v. 허가하다, 허락하다 (permission n. 허락, 허가)
If someone permit you to do something, they allow you to do it.

dumb[*]
[dʌm]

a. 멍청한, 바보 같은; 벙어리의, 말을 하지 않는
If you say that something is dumb, you think that it is silly and annoying.

stranger^{**}
[stréindʒər]

n. 낯선 사람, 모르는 사람
A stranger is someone you have never met before.

52

reluctant*
[rilʎktənt]

a. 꺼리는, 마지못해 하는, 주저하는 (reluctantly ad. 마지못해서, 꺼려하여)

If you are reluctant to do something, you are unwilling to do it and hesitate before doing it, or do it slowly and without enthusiasm.

1. Why did Bradley think that Jeff wouldn't have other friends?
   A. Jeff was new at the school and didn't know anyone.
   B. Jeff went to the see counselor, so the other kids thought he was weird.
   C. Bradley would beat up anyone else who wanted to be Jeff's friend.
   D. Nobody else would like him as long as Bradley was his friend.

2. What did Bradley think might happen if he did his homework?
   A. He might get a gold star.
   B. He might get a better grade.
   C. He might do well on a test.
   D. He might make his parents happy.

3. Why did Bradley want to beat up the girls?
   A. He wanted them to give him a dollar.
   B. He wanted them not to be friends with Jeff.
   C. He wanted them to stop saying hello to Jeff.
   D. He wanted them to like Jeff.

4. Which of the following was NOT something that Bradley said about fighting girls?
   A. They cry and run away after you hit them once.
   B. Girls hate it when their clothes get dirty.
   C. Girls kick, because they don't know how to punch.
   D. Girls are smaller than boys and easier to push over.

5. What did Bradley tell his mother had happened?
   A. He said that he had been beaten up by girls.
   B. He said that he had been beaten up and thrown in mud.
   C. He said that he accidentally fell in the mud on his way home.
   D. He said that a dog had jumped up on him.

6. Who did Bradley say beat him up?
   A. Melinda
   B. Jeff
   C. Robbie
   D. Colleen

7. What did Melinda ask Jeff and the girls to do after the fight?
   A. She asked them not to tell anyone about what happened.
   B. She asked them to help her apologize to Bradley.
   C. She asked them not to talk to Bradley again.
   D. She asked them to say that Jeff had punched Bradley.

1분에 몇 단어를 읽는지 리딩 속도를 측정해보세요.

$$\frac{379 \text{ words}}{\text{reading time ( ) sec}} \times 60 = (\qquad) \text{ WPM}$$

Build Your Vocabulary

drag[*]
[dræg]
v. 끌다, 힘들게 움직이다; n. 견인, 끌기
If you drag something, you pull it along the ground.

hall[복습]
[hɔːl]
n. (건물 안의) 복도; (건물 입구 안쪽의) 현관
A hall in a building is a long passage with doors into rooms on both sides of it.

appreciate[복습]
[əpriːʃièit]
v. 고맙게 생각하다; 평가하다, 감상하다
If you appreciate something that someone has done for you or is going to do for you, you are grateful for it.

doorway[*]
[dɔ́ːrwèi]
n. 출입구
A doorway is a space in a wall where a door opens and closes.

make sense[복습]
idiom 뜻이 통하다, 도리에 맞다
If something makes sense, it has a meaning that you can easily understand.

trust[**]
[trʌst]
v. 신뢰하다, 믿다; n. 신뢰, 신임
If you trust someone, you believe that they are honest and sincere and will not deliberately do anything to harm you.

deaf[*]
[def]
a. 귀가 먹은, 청각 장애가 있는
Someone who is deaf is unable to hear anything or is unable to hear very well.

let it go
idiom 그것으로 됐다, 그 이상 문제 삼지 않다
If you let it go, you say or do nothing more about something.

triangular[*]
[traiǽŋgjulər]
a. 삼각형인; 세 부분으로 된
Something that is triangular is in the shape of a triangle.

all the way[복습]
idiom 완전히; 내내
You can use all the way to emphasize that your remark applies to every part of a situation, activity, or period of time.

exclamation[*]
[èkskləméiʃən]
n. 감탄; 외침, 외치는 소리 (exclamation point n. 느낌표)
An exclamation is a sound, word, or sentence that is spoken suddenly, loudly, or emphatically and that expresses excitement, admiration, shock, or anger.

interrupt[복습]
[ìntərʌ́pt]
v. 방해하다, 가로막다, 저지하다
If you interrupt someone who is speaking, you say or do something that causes them to stop.

56

1분에 몇 단어를 읽는지 리딩 속도를 측정해보세요.

$$\frac{751 \text{ words}}{\text{reading time ( ) sec}} \times 60 = (\qquad) \text{ WPM}$$

Build Your Vocabulary

row^{복습}
[rou]
① n. 열, 줄 ② v. 노를 젓다, 배를 젓다; n. 노 젓기
A row of things or people is a number of them arranged in a line.

reason*
① v. 판단하다, 추론하다; n. 이유, 까닭
If you reason that something is true, you decide that it is true after thinking carefully about all the facts.

scribble^{복습}
[skribl]
v. 낙서하다; 갈겨쓰다, 휘갈기다; n. 낙서
To scribble means to make meaningless marks or rough drawings using a pencil or pen.

beat^{복습}
[bi:t]
v. 치다, 두드리다; 패배시키다, 이기다; (심장이) 고동치다; n. [음악] 박자, 고동
If you beat someone or something, you hit them very hard.

hop^{복습}
[hap]
v. 깡충 뛰다, 뛰어오르다; n. 깡충깡충 뜀
If you hop, you move along by jumping.

drizzle^{복습}
[drizl]
n. 이슬비, 가랑비; v. 이슬비가 내리다
Drizzle is light rain falling in fine drops.

sneak^{복습}
[sni:k]
v. 살금살금 가다, 몰래 가다
If you sneak somewhere, you go there very quietly on foot, trying to avoid being seen or heard.

assure^{복습}
[əʃúər]
v. 단언하다, 확신하다, 보증하다
If you assure someone that something is true or will happen, you tell them that it is definitely true or will definitely happen, often in order to make them less worried.

right away^{복습}
idiom 곧바로, 즉시
If you do something right away, you do it immediately.

barely*
[béərli]
ad. 간신히, 가까스로; 거의 ~않다
You use barely to say that something is only just true or only just the case.

mist*
[mist]
v. 이슬비가 내리다; 안개가 끼다, (창문 · 눈이) 흐려지다; n. 안개
If it is misting, it is raining in very fine drops or drizzling.

neat*
[ni:t]
a. 말끔한, 깔끔한; 멋진, 훌륭한 (neatly ad. 깔끔하게)
A neat place, thing, or person is tidy and smart, and has everything in the correct place.

disgust*
[disgʌst]

v. 역겹게 하다, 넌더리나게 하다; n. 싫음, 혐오감 (disgusting a. 역겨운, 불쾌한)
To disgust someone means to make them feel a strong sense of dislike and disapproval.

distance**
[dístəns]

n. 거리, 먼 거리; v. 간격을 두다, 멀리 놓다
If you keep your distance from someone or something, you do not get physically close to them.

sidewalk^{복습}
[sáidwɔːk]

n. (포장한) 보도, 인도
A sidewalk is a path with a hard surface by the side of a road.

warn^{복습}
[wɔːrn]

v. 경고하다; ~에게 통지하다
If you warn someone about something such as a possible danger or problem, you tell them about it so that they are aware of it.

quicken*
[kwíkən]

v. 더 빠르게 하다, 서두르다, 빨라지다
If something quickens or if you quicken it, it becomes faster or moves at a greater speed.

pace*
[peis]

n. 걷는 속도; 걸음걸이
Your pace is the speed at which you walk.

lag
[læg]

v. 뒤에 처지다, 뒤떨어지다
If one thing or person lags behind another thing or person, their progress is slower than that of the other.

make a face^{복습}

idiom 얼굴을 찌푸리다
If you make a face, you twist your face to indicate a certain mental or emotional state.

snap^{복습}
[snæp]

v. (화난 목소리로) 딱딱거리다; 딱[툭] (하고) 부러뜨리다, 부러지다
If someone snaps at you, they speak to you in a sharp, unfriendly way.

shove^{복습}
[ʃʌv]

v. 밀치다, 떠밀다; (아무렇게나) 밀어넣다; n. 밀치기
If you shove someone or something, you push them with a quick, violent movement.

slip^{복습}
[slip]

v. 미끄러지다; 살짝 나오다, 살짝 들어가다
If you slip, you accidentally slide and lose your balance.

hysterical
[histérikəl]

a. 히스테리 상태의, 발작적인 (hysterically ad. 흥분하여)
Hysterical laughter is loud and uncontrolled.

scramble*
[skræmbl]

v. 재빨리 움직이다, (민첩하게) 기어오르다; 뒤섞다; n. 기어오르기
If you scramble to a different place or position, you move there in a hurried, awkward way.

tease^{복습}
[tiːz]

v. 놀리다, 장난하다; n. 장난, 놀림
To tease someone means to laugh at them or make jokes about them in order to embarrass, annoy, or upset them.

yell^{복습}
[jel]

v. 소리치다, 고함치다; n. 고함소리, 부르짖음
If you yell, you shout loudly, usually because you are excited, angry, or in pain.

punch^{복습}
[pʌntʃ]

v. 주먹으로 치다, 때리다; n. 주먹으로 한 대 침, 펀치
If you punch someone or something, you hit them hard with your fist.

fist ^{복습}
[fist]

n. (쥔) 주먹
Your hand is referred to as your fist when you have bent your fingers in toward the palm in order to hit someone, to make an angry gesture, or to hold something.

charge^{**}
[ʧɑːrdʒ]

v. 돌격하다, 돌진하다; 청구하다; n. 요금; 책임
If you charge toward someone or something, you move quickly and aggressively toward them.

slug
[slʌg]

v. (주먹으로) 세게 때리다, 강타하다
If you slug someone, you hit them hard.

might^{**}
[mait]

n. 힘, 완력; 세력, 권력 (with all one's might **idiom** 전력을 다하여, 힘껏)
Might is power or strength.

stumble[*]
[stʌmbl]

v. 비틀거리며 걷다, 발부리가 걸리다; n. 비틀거림
If you stumble, you put your foot down awkwardly while you are walking or running and nearly fall over.

glare ^{복습}
[glɛər]

v. 노려보다; 번쩍번쩍 빛나다; n. 노려봄; 섬광
If you glare at someone, you look at them with an angry expression on your face.

swell[*]
[swel]

v. 솟아나다, 넘치다; 붓다, 팽창하다; n. 팽창, 증대
If a liquid as a spring or tears swells, it wells up.

tear ^{복습}
[tiəːr]

① n. 눈물 ② v. 부리나케 가다; 찢다, 찢어지다; n. 찢음
Tears are the drops of salty liquid that come out of your eyes when you are crying.

Check Your Reading Speed

1분에 몇 단어를 읽는지 리딩 속도를 측정해보세요.

$$\frac{665 \text{ words}}{\text{reading time (} \quad \text{) sec}} \times 60 = (\quad) \text{ WPM}$$

Build Your Vocabulary

wrap[**]
[ræp]

v. 감싸다; 포장하다; n. 싸개, 덮개
If someone wraps their arms, fingers, or legs around something, they put them firmly around it.

massive[*]
[mǽsiv]

a. 거대한, 육중한
Something that is massive is very large in size, quantity, or extent.

sob[*]
[sab]

v. 흐느껴 울다; n. 흐느낌, 오열
When someone sobs, they cry in a noisy way, breathing in short breaths.

wipe[*]
[waip]

v. 닦다, 닦아 내다; n. 닦기
If you wipe something, you rub its surface to remove dirt or liquid from it.

sleeve[복습]
[sli:v]

n. (옷의) 소매, 소맷자락
The sleeves of a coat, shirt, or other item of clothing are the parts that cover your arms.

comb[*]
[koum]

v. (머리카락 · 동물의 털 따위를) 빗질하다, 빗다; n. 빗
When you comb your hair, you tidy it using a comb.

bully[*]
[búli]

n. 약자를 괴롭히는 사람; v. 곯리다, 겁주다
A bully is someone who uses their strength or power to hurt or frighten other people.

pick on

idiom (구어) 괴롭히다, 못살게 굴다; ~을 선택하다, 고르다
If you pick on someone, you treat someone badly or unfairly, especially repeatedly.

rip[*]
[rip]

v. 찢다, 벗겨내다; n. 찢어진 틈, 잡아 찢음
When something rips or when you rip it, you tear it forcefully with your hands or with a tool such as a knife.

accuse[복습]
[əkjú:z]

v. 비난하다, 고발하다
If you accuse someone of doing something wrong or dishonest, you say or tell them that you believe that they did it.

lay[***]
[lei]

v. (laid–laid) 놓다, 눕히다; 알을 낳다
If you lay something somewhere, you put it there in a careful, gentle, or neat way.

counter[복습]
[káuntər]

n. 긴 테이블; 계산대; (부엌의) 조리대; v. 반박하다
A counter is a long narrow table or flat surface.

60

in the nick of time

idiom 마침 제때에, 때마침
If you say that something happens in the nick of time, you are emphasizing that it happens at the last possible moment.

romp
[ramp]

v. 떠들썩하게 뛰놀다; n. 떠들며 뛰어놀기
When children or animals romp, they play noisily and happily.

chase^{복습}
[ʧeis]

v. 뒤쫓다; 추구하다; 쫓아내다; n. 추적, 추격
If you chase someone, or chase after them, you run after them or follow them quickly in order to catch or reach them.

edge^{복습}
[edʒ]

n. 가장자리, 변두리, 끝; v. 조금씩[살살] 움직이다; 테두리를 두르다
The edge of something is the place or line where it stops, or the part of it that is furthest from the middle.

cliff**
[klif]

n. 절벽, 낭떠러지
A cliff is a high area of land with a very steep side, especially one next to the sea.

trap*
[træp]

v. 좁은 장소에 가두다; 함정에 빠뜨리다; n. 덫, 함정
If you are trapped somewhere, something falls onto you or blocks your way and prevents you from moving or escaping.

move in^{복습}

idiom (위협적으로) 사방에서 접근하다; 이사를 들다
If you move in, you to move toward someone or something, especially in a threatening way.

tremble^{복습}
[trembl]

v. 떨다, 떨리다 (trembling a. 떠는, 떨리는)
If you tremble, you shake slightly because you are frightened or cold.

attack***
[ətǽk]

v. 공격하다, 습격하다; n. 공격; 발작
To attack a person or place means to try to hurt or damage them using physical violence.

stomach**
[stʌ́mək]

n. 배, 복부; 위
You can refer to the front part of your body below your waist as your stomach.

flip*
[flip]

v. 튕겨 올리다, 홱 뒤집다; (책 등을) 휙휙 넘기다; n. 손가락으로 튕김
If something flips over, or if you flip it over or into a different position, it moves or is moved into a different position.

swing^{복습}
[swiŋ]

v. 휘두르다; (한 점을 축으로 하여) 빙 돌다, 휙 움직이다
If something swings in a particular direction or if you swing it in that direction, it moves in that direction with a smooth, curving movement.

axe*
[æks]

n. (= ax) 도끼; v. 도끼로 자르다
An axe is a tool used for cutting wood which consists of a heavy metal blade.

chop^{복습}
[ʧap]

v. 자르다, 잘게 썰다; n. 절단; 잘라낸 조각
If you chop something, you cut it into pieces with strong downward movements of a knife or an ax.

sneer
[sniər]

v. 비웃다, 냉소하다; n. 비웃음, 냉소
If you sneer at someone or something, you express your contempt for them by the expression on your face or by what you say.

duck ^{복습}
[dʌk]

① v. 피하다, 머리를 홱 숙이다 ② n. 오리

If you duck, you move your head or the top half of your body quickly downward to avoid something that might hit you, or to avoid being seen.

declare ^{복습}
[dikléər]

v. 단언하다; 선언하다

If you declare that something is true, you say that it is true in a firm, deliberate way.

shrug ^{복습}
[ʃrʌg]

v. (양 손바닥을 내보이면서 어깨를) 으쓱하다; n. 으쓱하기

If you shrug, you raise your shoulders to show that you are not interested in something or that you do not know or care about something.

chip ^{복습}
[ʧip]

n. 조각, 토막; v. 깨지다, 이가 빠지다; 잘게 썰다

A chip is a small piece of something or a small piece which has been broken off something.

lick*
[lik]

v. 핥다; n. 한 번 핥기, 핥아먹기

When people or animals lick something, they move their tongue across its surface.

principal ^{복습}
[prínsəpəl]

n. 장(長), 교장; a. 주요한, 제1의

The principal of a school or a college, is the person in charge of the school or college.

gang*
[gæŋ]

n. 패거리, 한 떼, 무리

A gang is a group of people who go around together and often deliberately cause trouble.

Check Your Reading Speed

1분에 몇 단어를 읽는지 리딩 속도를 측정해보세요.

$$\frac{699 \text{ words}}{\text{reading time ( ) sec}} \times 60 = (\quad) \text{ WPM}$$

Build Your Vocabulary

scare^{복습}
[skɛər]

v. 위협하다, 겁나게 하다 (scared a. 무서워하는, 겁먹은)
If something scares you, it frightens or worries you.

bully^{복습}
[búli]

n. 약자를 괴롭히는 사람; v. 굴리다, 겁주다
A bully is someone who uses their strength or power to hurt or frighten other people.

terrorize
[térəràiz]

v. 위협하다, 공포의 도가니로 몰아넣다
If someone terrorizes you, they keep you in a state of fear by making it seem likely that they will attack you.

baby***
[béibi]

v. 어린애 취급하다, 귀여워하다; n. 아기
To baby someone means to treat them like a young child.

stand up for

idiom 옹호하다, 지지하다
If you stand up for yourself, you support or defend yourself, especially when someone is criticizing you.

pick on^{복습}

idiom (부당하게) ~을 괴롭히다; ~을 선택하다
If you pick on someone, you treat someone badly or unfairly, especially repeatedly.

cautious*
[kɔ́ːʃəs]

a. 조심성 있는, 신중한 (cautiously ad. 조심스럽게)
Someone who is cautious acts very carefully in order to avoid possible danger.

schoolyard
[skúːljàːrd]

n. 교정, 학교 운동장
The schoolyard is the large open area with a hard surface just outside a school building, where the schoolchildren can play and do other activities.

adjective*
[ǽdʒiktiv]

n. 형용사; a. 부수적인, 형용사의
An adjective is a word such as 'big', 'dead', or 'financial' that describes a person or thing, or gives extra information about them.

adverb*
[ǽdvəːrb]

n. 부사; a. 부사적인, 부사의
An adverb is a word such as 'slowly', 'now', 'very', 'politically', or 'fortunately' which adds information about the action, event, or situation mentioned in a clause.

race^{복습}
[reis]

① v. 질주하다, 달리다; 경주하다; n. 경주 ② n. 인종, 민족
If your mind races, or if thoughts race through your mind, you think very fast about something, especially when you are in a difficult or dangerous situation.

stick ^{복습}
[stik]

① v. (stuck-stuck) 붙이다, 달라붙다; 내밀다; 찔러 넣다, 찌르다
② n. 막대기, 지팡이
If one thing sticks to another, it becomes attached to it and is difficult to remove.

glue ^{복습}
[glu:]

v. 풀로 붙이다, 접착하다; n. 풀, 접착제
If you glue one object to another, you stick them together using glue.

accidental ^{복습}
[æksədéntl]

a. 우연한; 부수적인 (accidentally ad. 우연히)
An accidental event happens by chance or as the result of an accident, and is not deliberately intended.

grab ^{복습}
[græb]

v. 부여잡다, 움켜쥐다; n. 부여잡기
If you grab something, you take it or pick it up suddenly and roughly.

wrist *
[rist]

n. 손목
Your wrist is the part of your body between your hand and your arm which bends when you move your hand.

pretend ^{복습}
[priténd]

v. ~인 체하다, 가장하다; a. 가짜의, 꾸민
If you pretend that something is the case, you act in a way that is intended to make people believe that it is the case, although in fact it is not.

unstick
[ʌnstik]

v. (달라붙은 것을) 잡아떼다
If you unstick something or if it unsticks, it becomes separated from the thing that it was stuck to.

loosen *
[lu:sn]

v. 풀다, 느슨해지다
If you loosen your clothing or something that is tied or fastened or if it loosens, you undo it slightly so that it is less tight or less firmly held in place.

pry
[prai]

① v. 비틀어 움직이다; 지레로 들어 올리다; n. 지레 ② v. 엿보다, 동정을 살피다
If you pry something open or pry it away from a surface, you force it open or away from the surface.

bluish
[blu:iʃ]

a. 푸르스름한, 푸른빛을 띤
Something that is bluish is slightly blue in color.

stare ^{복습}
[stɛər]

v. 응시하다, 뚫어지게 보다
If you stare at someone or something, you look at them for a long time.

recess ^{복습}
[rí:ses]

n. (학교의) 쉬는 시간; 휴회
A recess is a short period of time when you have a rest or a change from what you are doing, especially if you are working or if you are in a boring or unpleasant situation.

bother ^{복습}
[báðər]

v. 귀찮게 하다, 괴롭히다; 일부러 ~하다, 애를 쓰다
If someone bothers you, they talk to you when you want to be left alone or interrupt you when you are busy.

spread ***

v. (spread-spread) 퍼지다, 퍼뜨리다; 펴다, 펼치다
If something spreads or is spread by people, it gradually reaches or affects a larger and larger area or more and more people.

wander[*]
[wándər]

v. 돌아다니다, 방황하다; n. 유랑, 방랑

If you wander in a place, you walk around there in a casual way, often without intending to go in any particular direction.

peek[복습]
[pi:k]

n. 엿봄; v. 살짝 들여다보다, 엿보다

A peek is a quick look at something or someone.

impolite[*]
[ìmpəláit]

a. 무례한, 실례되는

If you say that someone is impolite, you mean that they are rather rude and do not have good manners.

1. Why did the boys invite Jeff to play basketball?

    A. They didn't want Jeff hanging out with Bradley.

    B. They thought that Jeff gave Bradley the black eye.

    C. They thought that Jeff could be a good player.

    D. They needed another player to make the teams even.

2. How did Jeff treat Bradley after the basketball game?

    A. He offered to do homework with Bradley.

    B. He still treated Bradley like a friend.

    C. He invited Bradley to play with them all.

    D. He ignored Bradley in class.

3. What did Bradley want to do together with Jeff after school?

    A. He wanted to sneak into the girls' bathroom.

    B. He wanted to play basketball.

    C. He wanted to do homework.

    D. He wanted to talk to Carla.

4. How did Bradley feel about his friendship with Jeff?

    A. He had just been pretending to be his friend.

    B. He had really been his best friend.

    C. He realized that he was better off with a friend.

    D. He realized that he had felt sorry for Jeff.

5. What did Jeff tell Carla about Bradley?
   A. He told her that Bradley spit on him.
   B. He told her that he gave Bradley his black eye.
   C. He told her that Bradley went inside the girls' bathroom.
   D. He told her that Bradley hated her.

6. Why did Jeff say he would stop seeing Carla?
   A. He said that it was because he was moving to a new school.
   B. He said that it was because he wasn't friends with Bradley anymore.
   C. He said that it was because he didn't have time anymore.
   D. He said that it was because he had eight friends now.

7. How did Colleen's parents feel about Carla?
   A. They said that she was helpful for other students.
   B. They said that Colleen already had another counselor.
   C. They said that the school should have hired her earlier.
   D. They said that hiring her was a waste of money.

1분에 몇 단어를 읽는지 리딩 속도를 측정해보세요.

$$\frac{374 \text{ words}}{\text{reading time ( ) sec}} \times 60 = (\quad) \text{ WPM}$$

Build Your Vocabulary

recognize**
[rékəgnaiz]

v. 인지하다, 알아보다
If you recognize someone or something, you know who that person is or what that thing is.

captain**
[kǽptən]

n. (운동팀의) 주장; 우두머리, 장(長)
The captain of a sports team is the player in charge of it.

beam*
[biːm]

v. 활짝 웃다; 비추다; n. 환한 얼굴; 빛줄기; [건축] 들보, 기둥
If you say that someone is beaming, you mean that they have a big smile on their face because they are happy, pleased, or proud about something.

remainder*
[riméindər]

n. 나머지, 잔여 부분
The remainder of a group are the things or people that still remain after the other things or people have gone or have been dealt with.

period^{복습}
[píːəriəd]

n. 시간, 기간; 시기, 시대
A period is a length of time.

hang around with

idiom ~와 많은 시간을 보내다
If you hang around with someone or with a group of people, you spend a lot of time with them.

Check Your Reading Speed

1분에 몇 단어를 읽는지 리딩 속도를 측정해보세요.

$$\frac{416 \text{ words}}{\text{reading time (} \quad \text{) sec}} \times 60 = (\quad) \text{ WPM}$$

Build Your Vocabulary

brick**
[brik]

n. 벽돌; v. 벽돌로 막다
Bricks are rectangular blocks of baked clay used for building walls, which are usually red or brown.

shot**
[ʃat]

n. 시도, 기회; 겨냥, 발사; 주사
If you have a shot at something, you attempt to do it.

pray**
[prei]

v. 기원하다, 빌다
When people pray, they speak to God in order to give thanks or to ask for his help.

row복습
[rou]

① n. 열, 줄 ② v. 노를 젓다, 배를 젓다; n. 노 젓기
A row of things or people is a number of them arranged in a line.

intent*
[intént]

① a. 집중된, 열심인, 여념이 없는 (intently ad. 골똘하게) ② n. 의지, 의향
If you are intent on doing something, you are eager and determined to do it.

principal복습
[prínsəpəl]

n. 장(長), 교장; a. 주요한, 제1의
The principal of a school or a college, is the person in charge of the school or college.

whisper복습
[hwíspər]

v. 속삭이다
When you whisper, you say something very quietly.

hooray**
[huréi]

int. 만세; v. 만세를 부르다
People sometimes shout 'Hooray!' when they are very happy and excited about something.

hippopotamus
[hipəpátəməs]

n. (= hippo) [동물] 하마
A hippopotamus is a very large African animal with short legs and thick, hairless skin.

yell복습
[jel]

v. 소리치다, 고함치다; n. 고함소리, 부르짖음
If you yell, you shout loudly, usually because you are excited, angry, or in pain.

donkey복습
[dánki]

n. [동물] 당나귀
A donkey is an animal which is like a horse but which is smaller and has longer ears.

ivory복습
[áivəri]

a. 상아로 만든; 상아색의; n. 상아
An ivory thing is made of a hard cream-colored substance which forms the tusks of elephants.

Check Your Reading Speed

1분에 몇 단어를 읽는지 리딩 속도를 측정해보세요.

$$\frac{500 \text{ words}}{\text{reading time (} \quad \text{) sec}} \times 60 = (\quad) \text{ WPM}$$

Build Your Vocabulary

normal**
[nɔ́:rməl]

a. 보통의, 정상의, 평범한
Something that is normal is usual and ordinary, and is what people expect.

scribble복습
[skríbl]

v. 낙서하다; 갈겨쓰다, 휘갈기다; n. 낙서
To scribble means to make meaningless marks or rough drawings using a pencil or pen.

cut something up복습

idiom ~을 조각조각[잘게] 자르다
If you cut something up, you divide something into small pieces with a knife or a tool.

tape복습
[teip]

v. (접착) 테이프로 붙이다; 녹음하다, 녹화하다;
n. (소리 · 영상을 기록하는) 테이프; (접착용) 테이프
If you tape one thing to another, you attach it using sticky strip of plastic.

shudder*
[ʃʌ́dər]

v. 떨다, 몸서리치다; n. 떨림, 전율
If you shudder, you shake with fear, horror, or disgust, or because you are cold.

horrible복습
[hɔ́:rəbl]

a. 끔찍한, 소름 끼치게 싫은; 무서운
You can call something horrible when it causes you to feel great shock, fear, and disgust.

be better off

idiom 더 좋은 상태이다, ~하는 편이 낫다
Be better off is used to say that someone is or would be happier or more satisfied if they were in a particular position or did a particular thing.

pretend복습
[priténd]

v. ~인 체하다, 가장하다; a. 가짜의, 꾸민
If you pretend that something is the case, you act in a way that is intended to make people believe that it is the case, although in fact it is not.

announce복습
[ənáuns]

v. 발표하다, 알리다
If you announce a piece of news or an intention, especially something that people may not like, you say it loudly and clearly, so that everyone you are with can hear it.

consider***
[kənsídər]

v. 고려하다, 숙고하다; ~라고 여기다
If you consider something, you think about it carefully.

quality복습
[kwáləti]

n. 질, 품질; 성질, 특성; 소질, 재능
The quality of something is how good or bad it is.

70

quantity^{**}
[kwántiti]

n. 양, 분량
A quantity is an amount that you can measure or count.

when it comes to

idiom ~에 관하여, ~에 관해서라면
When it comes to something or to doing something is used to when it is a case or matter of it.

glance^{복습}
[glæns]

v. 흘긋 보다, 잠깐 보다; n. 흘긋 봄
If you glance at something or someone, you look at them very quickly and then look away again immediately.

bother^{복습}
[báðər]

v. 귀찮게 하다, 괴롭히다; 일부러 ~하다, 애를 쓰다
If someone bothers you, they talk to you when you want to be left alone or interrupt you when you are busy.

hang around^{복습}

idiom (~에서) 서성거리다
If you hang around, you spend time somewhere, without doing very much.

spit^{복습}
[spit]

v. (침 등을) 뱉다; 내뱉듯이 말하다; n. 침
If someone spits, they force an amount of liquid out of their mouth, often to show hatred or contempt.

threaten^{복습}
[θretn]

v. 위협하다, 협박하다; 조짐을 보이다
If a person threatens to do something unpleasant to you, or if they threaten you, they say or imply that they will do something unpleasant to you, especially if you do not do what they want.

get away with

idiom 처벌을 모면하다, 그냥 넘어가다
If you get away with doing something, you do something wrong and are not punished or criticized for it.

duck^{복습}
[dʌk]

① v. 피하다, 머리를 홱 숙이다 ② n. 오리
If you duck, you move your head or the top half of your body quickly downward to avoid something that might hit you, or to avoid being seen.

punch^{복습}
[pʌntʃ]

v. 주먹으로 치다, 때리다; n. 주먹으로 한 대 침, 펀치
If you punch someone or something, you hit them hard with your fist.

counsel^{복습}
[káunsəl]

v. 상담을 하다; n. 조언, 충고 (counselor n. 지도교사, 상담사)
If you counsel people, you give them advice about their problems.

weird^{복습}
[wiərd]

a. 이상한, 기묘한; 수상한
If you describe something or someone as weird, you mean that they are strange.

nod^{복습}
[nad]

v. 끄덕이다, 끄덕여 표시하다; n. (동의 · 인사 · 신호 · 명령의) 끄덕임
If you nod, you move your head downward and upward to show agreement, understanding, or approval.

chuckle[*]
[tʃʌkl]

v. 빙그레 웃다, 소리 없이 웃다
When you chuckle, you laugh quietly.

accidental^{복습}
[æksədéntl]

a. 우연한; 부수적인 (accidentally ad. 우연히)
An accidental event happens by chance or as the result of an accident, and is not deliberately intended.

jerk[*]
[dʒəːrk]

n. 바보, 얼간이; 갑자기 잡아당김; v. 갑자기 움직이다
If you call someone a jerk, you are insulting them because you think they are stupid or you do not like them.

stretch[복습]
[stretʃ]

v. 늘이다; 늘어지다; 기지개를 켜다; (팔·다리의 근육을) 당기다; n. 기지개 켜기
When something soft or elastic stretches or is stretched, it becomes longer or bigger as well as thinner, usually because it is pulled.

frown[복습]
[fraun]

n. 찌푸린 얼굴; v. 얼굴을 찡그리다. 눈살을 찌푸리다
A frown is a look that your face makes with your eyebrows drawn together because you are annoyed or puzzled.

1분에 몇 단어를 읽는지 리딩 속도를 측정해보세요.

$$\frac{318 \text{ words}}{\text{reading time ( ) sec}} \times 60 = (\qquad) \text{ WPM}$$

Build Your Vocabulary

waste**
[weist]

n. 낭비, 허비; v. 낭비하다; a. 쓸모없는, 버려진
Waste is the use of money or other resources on things that do not need it.

hire복습
[haiər]

v. 고용하다; 빌리다, 빌려주다; n. 고용
If you hire someone, you employ them or pay them to do a particular job for you.

shrug복습
[ʃrʌg]

v. (양 손바닥을 내보이면서 어깨를) 으쓱하다; n. 으쓱하기
If you shrug, you raise your shoulders to show that you are not interested in something or that you do not know or care about something.

sigh복습
[sai]

v. 한숨 쉬다; n. 한숨, 탄식
When you sigh, you let out a deep breath, as a way of expressing feelings such as disappointment, tiredness, or pleasure.

assure복습
[əʃûər]

v. 단언하다, 확신하다, 보증하다
If you assure someone that something is true or will happen, you tell them that it is definitely true or will definitely happen, often in order to make them less worried.

scare복습
[skɛər]

v. 위협하다, 겁나게 하다 (scared a. 무서워하는, 겁먹은)
If something scares you, it frightens or worries you.

1. How did Bradley tell Carla that he got a black eye?
   A. He said that Melinda punched him.
   B. He said that Jeff punched him.
   C. He said that he punched himself.
   D. He said that it was just makeup.

2. What did Bradley say would happen if he talked about school?
   A. He said that he would throw up.
   B. He said that he would die.
   C. He said that he would cry.
   D. He said that he would get angry.

3. What did Bradley write on his list three times?
   A. Jobs
   B. Chalk
   C. Monsters
   D. Gold stars

4. What did Claudia say was the reason for Carla listening to Bradley?
   A. She said that Carla listened to Bradley, because it was her job to listen.
   B. She said that Carla listened to Bradley, because she liked Bradley.

C. She said that Carla listened to Bradley, because Bradley had
interesting things to say.

D. She said that Carla listened to Bradley, because she always
listened to anyone.

5. How did Carla feel about monsters?
   A. She believed in monsters and had nightmares about them.
   B. She believed in monsters and thought they were ugly and scary.
   C. She didn't believe in monsters and thought everyone had 'good' in
   them.
   D. She didn't believe in monsters but thought some people only had
   'bad' inside them.

6. Which of the following did NOT happen when Jeff met
Colleen and her friends after school?
   A. Colleen invited Jeff to her birthday party.
   B. Jeff told them to stop saying hello to him.
   C. Melinda punched and beat up Jeff.
   D. Lori made a mistake and said 'Jello, Jeff' instead of 'Hello, Jeff.'

7. How was making a list of topics to discuss with Carla the
opposite of homework?
   A. It was the opposite of homework, because he didn't have to read a
   book.
   B. It was the opposite of homework, because he didn't write
   anything down.
   C. It was the opposite of homework, because it was work that he
   only did at school.
   D. It was the opposite of homework, because he wouldn't have to
   talk about homework.

Check Your Reading Speed

1분에 몇 단어를 읽는지 리딩 속도를 측정해보세요.

$$\frac{1{,}002 \text{ words}}{\text{reading time } (\quad) \text{ sec}} \times 60 = (\qquad) \text{ WPM}$$

Build Your Vocabulary

appreciate^{복습}
[əpríːʃièit]

v. 고맙게 생각하다; 평가하다, 감상하다
If you appreciate something that someone has done for you or is going to do for you, you are grateful for it.

beat^{복습}
[biːt]

v. 치다, 두드리다; 패배시키다, 이기다; (심장이) 고동치다; n. [음악] 박자, 고동
If you beat someone or something, you hit them very hard.

mouse^{복습}
[maus]

n. (pl. mice) [동물] 쥐, 생쥐
A mouse is a small furry animal with a long tail.

stare^{복습}
[stɛər]

v. 응시하다, 뚫어지게 보다
If you stare at someone or something, you look at them for a long time.

trick^{복습}
[trik]

n. 속임수; 비결, 요령; 묘기, 재주; v. 속이다, 속임수를 쓰다
A trick is an action that is intended to deceive someone.

glare^{복습}
[glɛər]

v. 노려보다; 번쩍번쩍 빛나다; n. 노려봄; 섬광
If you glare at someone, you look at them with an angry expression on your face.

quality^{복습}
[kwáləti]

n. 소질, 재능; 질, 품질; 성질, 특성
Someone's qualities are the good characteristics that they have which are part of their nature.

throw up^{복습}

idiom ~을 토하다, 게우다
When someone throws up, they bring food they have eaten back out of mouth.

lock**
[lak]

v. 잠그다; 고정시키다; 가두어 넣다; n. 자물쇠
When you lock something such as a door, drawer, or case, you fasten it, usually with a key, so that other people cannot open it.

swallow^{복습}
[swálou]

v. 삼키다, 목구멍으로 넘기다; (초조해서) 마른침을 삼키다
If you swallow something, you cause it to go from your mouth down into your stomach.

admit^{복습}
[ædmít]

v. 인정하다
If you admit that something bad, unpleasant, or embarrassing is true, you agree, often unwillingly, that it is true.

shift*
[ʃift]

v. 방향을 바꾸다, 옮기다; n. 변화, 이동; 교대
If you shift something or if it shifts, it moves slightly.

dart*
[da:rt]

v. (시선 · 화살 · 빛 등을) 던지다, 쏘다; 돌진하다; n. 던지는 화살, 다트
If you dart a look at someone or something, or if your eyes dart to them, you look at them very quickly.

restless*
[réstlis]

a. 침착하지 못한, 가만히 있지 못하는 (restlessly ad. 차분하지 못하게, 쉴없이)
If someone is restless, they keep moving around because they find it difficult to keep still.

lean복습
[li:n]

① v. 기울다, 기울이다, (몸을) 숙이다; ~에 기대다; ~을 ~에 기대 놓다
When you lean in a particular direction, you bend your body in that direction.

fold***
[fould]

v. (손 · 팔 · 다리를) 끼다, 포개다; 접다, 접어 포개다
If you fold your arms or hands, you bring them together and cross or link them, for example over your chest.

chin**
[tʃin]

n. 턱
Your chin is the part of your face that is below your mouth and above your neck.

nasty*
[nǽsti]

a. 심술궂은, 비열한; 더러운, 불쾌한
Something that is nasty is very unpleasant to see, experience, or feel.

fail***
[feil]

v. 실패하다, ~하지 못하다
If you fail to do something that you were trying to do, you are unable to do it or do not succeed in doing it.

hesitate복습
[hézətèit]

v. 주저하다, 머뭇거리다, 망설이다 (hesitatingly ad. 망설이며)
If you hesitate, you do not speak or act for a short time, usually because you are uncertain, embarrassed, or worried about what you are going to say or do.

assignment**
[əsáinmənt]

n. 숙제, 할당된 일, 임무
An assignment is a task or piece of work that you are given to do, especially as part of your job or studies.

on purpose복습

idiom 고의로, 일부러
If you do something on purpose, you do it intentionally.

grade복습
[greid]

n. 성적, 평점; 학년, 등급; v. 점수를 매기다, 등급을 매기다
Your grade in an examination or piece of written work is the mark you get, usually in the form of a letter or number, that indicates your level of achievement.

confidence**
[kánfədəns]

n. 신용, 신뢰; 자신(감), 확신
If you have confidence in someone, you feel that you can trust them.

discuss***
[diskʌ́s]

v. 토론하다, ~에 관하여 (서로) 이야기하다
If people discuss something, they talk about it, often in order to reach a decision.

risk***
[risk]

v. ~의 위험을 무릅쓰다; (~을) 위태롭게 하다; n. 위험
If you risk doing something, you do it, even though you know that it might have undesirable consequences.

stick^{복습}
[stik]

① v. (stuck–stuck) 찔러 넣다, 찌르다; 붙이다, 달라붙다; 내밀다
② n. 막대기, 지팡이

If you stick something somewhere, you put it there in a rather casual way.

1분에 몇 단어를 읽는지 리딩 속도를 측정해보세요.

$$\frac{988 \text{ words}}{\text{reading time (} \quad \text{) sec}} \times 60 = (\quad) \text{ WPM}$$

Build Your Vocabulary

discuss^{복습}
[diskʌ́s]

v. 토론하다, ~에 관하여 (서로) 이야기하다
If people discuss something, they talk about it, often in order to reach a decision.

opposite^{복습}
[ápəzit]

n. 정반대의 일; a. 반대편의, 맞은편의; 정반대의; ad. 정반대의 위치에
The opposite of someone or something is the person or thing that is most different from them.

recess^{복습}
[ríːses]

n. (학교의) 쉬는 시간; 휴회
A recess is a short period of time when you have a rest or a change from what you are doing, especially if you are working or if you are in a boring or unpleasant situation.

constant[*]
[kánstənt]

a. 끊임없는; 일정한, 불변의 (constantly ad. 끊임없이)
You use constant to describe something that happens all the time or is always there.

(be) on the lookout for

idiom (~이 있는지) 세심히 살피다, 지켜보다
If you are on the lookout for something or someone, you are searching for it or them.

call someone names

idiom ~를 욕하다
If someone calls you names, they insult you by saying unpleasant things to you or about you.

show off

idiom (실력 · 학식 등을) 자랑해 보이다; 돋보이게 하다
If you say that someone is showing off, you are criticizing them for trying to impress people by showing in a very obvious way what they can do or what they own.

outer space^{복습}
[áutər speis]

n. (대기권 외) 우주 공간
Outer space is the area outside the earth's atmosphere where the other planets and stars are situated.

chase^{복습}
[tʃeis]

v. 뒤쫓다; 추구하다; 쫓아내다; n. 추적, 추격
If you chase someone, or chase after them, you run after them or follow them quickly in order to catch or reach them.

costume[*]
[kástjuːm]

n. 의상, 옷차림
An actor's costume is the set of clothes they wear while they are performing.

allow^{복습}
[əláu]

v. 허락하다, ~하게 두다; 인정하다
If someone is allowed to do something, it is all right for them to do it and they will not get into trouble.

borrow***
[bárou]

v. (물건 · 돈 · 생각 등을) 빌리다
If you borrow something that belongs to someone else, you take it or use it for a period of time, usually with their permission.

chalk**
[tʃɔːk]

n. 분필, 초크
Chalk is small sticks of chalk, or a substance similar to chalk, used for writing or drawing with.

sheet**
[ʃiːt]

n. (종이) 한 장; (침대) 시트
A sheet of paper is a rectangular piece of paper.

sharpen^{복습}
[ʃáːrpən]

v. 날카롭게 하다, (날카롭게) 갈다 (pencil sharpener n. 연필깎이)
If you sharpen an object, you make its edge very thin or you make its end pointed.

military^{복습}
[mílitèri]

n. 군대, 군인들; a. 군사의, 무력의 (military school n. 육군 사관 학교)
The military are the armed forces of a country.

cane^{복습}
[kein]

n. 지팡이
A cane is a long thin stick with a curved or round top which you can use to support yourself when you are walking.

enemy**
[énəmi]

n. 적, 원수
If someone is your enemy, they hate you or want to harm you.

jail^{복습}
[dʒeil]

n. 교도소, 감옥
A jail is a place where criminals are kept in order to punish them, or where people waiting to be tried are kept.

peanut^{복습}
[píːnʌt]

n. 땅콩 (peanut butter n. 땅콩 버터)
Peanuts are small nuts that grow under the ground. Peanuts are often eaten as a snack, especially roasted and salted.

reflex^{복습}
[ríːfleks]

n. (pl. reflexes) 반사 작용, 반사 운동; a. 반사적인
A reflex or a reflex action is something that you do automatically and without thinking, as a habit or as a reaction to something.

beard*
[biərd]

n. (턱)수염
A man's beard is the hair that grows on his chin and cheeks.

closet^{복습}
[klázit]

n. 옷장, 벽장
A closet is a piece of furniture with doors at the front and shelves inside, which is used for storing things.

invisible*
[invízəbl]

a. 보이지 않는, 볼 수 없는
If you describe something as invisible, you mean that it cannot be seen, for example because it is transparent, hidden, or very small.

pirate*
[páiərət]

n. 해적, 해적선; 약탈자; v. 약탈하다
Pirates are sailors who attack other ships and steal property from them.

make fun of^{복습}

idiom ~을 놀리다, 웃음거리로 만들다
If you make fun of someone, you make unkind remarks or jokes them.

counsel^{복습}
[káunsəl]

v. 상담을 하다; n. 조언, 충고 (counselor n. 지도교사, 상담사)
If you counsel people, you give them advice about their problems.

80

barge into^{복습}
idiom 불쑥 들어오다, 불쑥 끼어들다
To barge into means to enter a place or join a group of people quickly and rudely, without being asked.

shove^{복습}
[ʃʌv]
v. (아무렇게나) 밀어넣다; 밀치다, 떠밀다; n. 밀치기
If you shove something somewhere, you push it there quickly and carelessly.

pillow^{복습}
[pílou]
n. 베개
A pillow is a rectangular cushion which you rest your head on when you are in bed.

flunk
[flʌŋk]
v. 실패하다, 낙제점을 받다; 단념하다, 그만두다
If you flunk an exam or a course, you fail to reach the required standard.

wander^{복습}
[wándər]
v. 돌아다니다, 방황하다; n. 유랑, 방랑
If you wander in a place, you walk around there in a casual way, often without intending to go in any particular direction.

lunge
[lʌndʒ]
v. 돌진하다, 달려들다; n. 돌입, 돌진
If you lunge in a particular direction, you move in that direction suddenly and clumsily.

dive**
[daiv]
v. 뛰어들다, 급히 움직이다; 다이빙하다
If you dive in a particular direction or into a particular place, you jump or move there quickly.

beat someone to it
idiom 기선을 제압하다, 선수를 치다
If you intend to do something but someone beats you to it, they do it before you do.

crack up
idiom 마구 웃기 시작하다
If you crack up, you start laughing a lot.

demand^{복습}
[dimǽnd]
v. 묻다, 요구하다, 청구하다; n. 요구, 수요
If you demand something such as information or action, you ask for it in a very forceful way.

stuff^{복습}
[stʌf]
n. 것(들), 물건, 물질; v. 채워 넣다, 속을 채우다
You can use stuff to refer to things such as a substance, a collection of things, events, or ideas in a general way without mentioning the thing itself by name.

insist^{복습}
[insíst]
v. 우기다, 주장하다; 강요하다
If you insist that something is the case, you say so very firmly and refuse to say otherwise, even though other people do not believe you.

grab^{복습}
[græb]
v. 부여잡다, 움켜쥐다; n. 부여잡기
If you grab something, you take it or pick it up suddenly and roughly.

scoff
[skɔːf]
v. 비웃다, 조소하다, 조롱하다; n. 비웃음, 조롱
If you scoff at something, you speak about it in a way that shows you think it is ridiculous or inadequate.

tear^{복습}
[tiəːr]
① n. 눈물 ② v. 부리나케 가다; 찢다, 찢어지다; n. 찢음
Tears are the drops of salty liquid that come out of your eyes when you are crying.

crumple ^{복습}
[krʌmpl]

v. 구기다, 쭈글쭈글하게 하다; 구겨지다; n. 주름

If you crumple something such as paper or cloth, or if it crumples, it is squashed and becomes full of untidy creases and folds.

1분에 몇 단어를 읽는지 리딩 속도를 측정해보세요.

$$\frac{1{,}187 \text{ words}}{\text{reading time ( ) sec}} \times 60 = (\quad) \text{ WPM}$$

Build Your Vocabulary

chubby
[ʧʌ́bi]

a. 토실토실 살찐, 오동통한
A chubby person is rather fat.

outer space^{복습}
[áutər speis]

n. (대기권 외) 우주 공간
Outer space is the area outside the earth's atmosphere where the other planets and stars are situated.

yell^{복습}
[jel]

v. 소리치다, 고함치다; n. 고함소리, 부르짖음
If you yell, you shout loudly, usually because you are excited, angry, or in pain.

skinny^{복습}
[skíni]

a. 바짝 여윈, 깡마른
A skinny person is extremely thin, often in a way that you find unattractive.

warn^{복습}
[wɔːrn]

v. 경고하다; ~에게 통지하다
If you warn someone about something such as a possible danger or problem, you tell them about it so that they are aware of it.

scatter^{**}
[skǽtər]

v. 뿔뿔이 흩어지다; 흩뿌리다, 뿌리다
If a group of people scatter or if you scatter them, they suddenly separate and move in different directions.

regroup
[riːgrúp]

v. (조직을) 재편성하다, 다시 모이다
When people, especially soldiers, regroup, or when someone regroups them, they form an organized group again, in order to continue fighting.

pigeon[*]
[pídʒən]

n. [동물] 비둘기
A pigeon is a bird, usually gray in color, which has a fat body.

row^{복습}
[rou]

① n. 열, 줄 ② v. 노를 젓다, 배를 젓다; n. 노 젓기
A row of things or people is a number of them arranged in a line.

hall^{복습}
[hɔːl]

n. (건물 안의) 복도; (건물 입구 안쪽의) 현관
A hall in a building is a long passage with doors into rooms on both sides of it.

sleeve^{복습}
[sliːv]

n. (옷의) 소매, 소맷자락 (long-sleeved a. 긴 소매의)
The sleeves of a coat, shirt, or other item of clothing are the parts that cover your arms.

discuss^{복습}
[diskʌ́s]

v. 토론하다, ~에 관하여 (서로) 이야기하다
If people discuss something, they talk about it, often in order to reach a decision.

come up with　idiom ~을 제안하다, ~을 내놓다
If you come up with a plan or idea, you think of it and suggest it.

ray[*]
[rei]　n. 광선, 빛; v. 번쩍이다 (ray gun n. (SF에 나오는) 광선총)
Rays of light are narrow beams of light.

grenade
[grinéid]　n. 수류탄
A grenade or a hand grenade is a small bomb that can be thrown by hand.

atomic[*]
[ətámik]　a. 원자의, 원자력에 의한 (atomic bomb n. 원자폭탄)
Atomic means relating to power that is produced from the energy released by splitting atoms.

bomb[**]
[bam]　n. 폭탄; v. 폭격하다, 폭발하다
A bomb is a device which explodes and damages or destroys a large area.

pretend[복습]
[priténd]　v. ~인 체하다, 가장하다; a. 가짜의, 꾸민
If you pretend that something is the case, you act in a way that is intended to make people believe that it is the case, although in fact it is not.

creature[**]
[kríːtʃər]　n. 생물, 창조물
You can refer to any living thing that is not a plant as a creature, especially when it is of an unknown or unfamiliar kind.

planet[*]
[plǽnit]　n. 행성
A planet is a large, round object in space that moves around a star.

gigantic[*]
[dʒaigǽntik]　a. 거대한, 막대한
If you describe something as gigantic, you are emphasizing that it is extremely large in size, amount, or degree.

universe[**]
[júːnivəːrs]　n. 우주; 전 세계
The universe is the whole of space and all the stars, planets, and other forms of matter and energy in it.

billion[***]
[bíljən]　n. 막대한 수; 10억
If you talk about billions of people or things, you mean that there is a very large number of them but you do not know or do not want to say exactly how many.

trillion[*]
[tríljən]　n. 1조(兆)
A trillion is a million million.

terrible[*]
[térəbl]　a. 무서운, 소름끼치는; 심한, 지독한
A terrible experience or situation is very serious or very unpleasant.

bury[**]
[béri]　v. 묻다, 파묻다, 매장하다
If something buries itself somewhere, or if you bury it there, it is pushed very deeply in there.

consider[복습]
[kənsídər]　v. ~라고 여기다; 고려하다, 숙고하다
If you consider a person or thing to be something, you have the opinion that this is what they are.

84

describe^{복습}
[diskráib]

v. 묘사하다, 기술하다; 평하다
If you describe a person, object, event, or situation, you say what they are like or what happened.

astonish*
[əstániʃ]

v. 깜짝 놀라게 하다 (astonishment n. 놀라움)
If something or someone astonishes you, they surprise you very much.

blush^{복습}
[blʌʃ]

v. 얼굴을 붉히다, (얼굴이) 빨개지다; n. 얼굴을 붉힘, 홍조
When you blush, your face becomes redder than usual because you are ashamed or embarrassed.

mumble^{복습}
[mʌmbl]

v. 중얼거리다, 웅얼거리다; n. 중얼거림
If you mumble, you speak very quietly and not at all clearly with the result that the words are difficult to understand.

conversation**
[kànvərséiʃən]

n. 대화, 회담
If you have a conversation with someone, you talk with them, usually in an informal situation.

session^{복습}
[séʃən]

n. (특정한 활동을 위한) 시간, 기간; 회의, 회기
A session of a particular activity is a period of that activity.

fit^{복습}
[fit]

v. 끼우다; (모양 · 크기가 어떤 사람 · 사물에) 맞다; 적절하다
If you fit something into a particular space or place, you put it there.

tack
[tæk]

v. 압정으로 고정시키다; n. 압정
If you tack something to a surface, you pin it there with tacks or drawing pins.

look forward to^{복습}

idiom ~을 고대하다
To look forward to means to feel excited about something that is going to happen because you expect to enjoy it.

light***
[lait]

v. (lit/lighted–lit/lighted) (빛을) 비추다; 불을 붙이다; n. 빛; a. (날이) 밝은
If a person's eyes or face light up, or something lights them up, they become bright with excitement or happiness.

stretch^{복습}
[stretʃ]

v. 늘이다; 늘어지다; 기지개를 켜다; (팔 · 다리의 근육을) 당기다; n. 기지개 켜기
When something soft or elastic stretches or is stretched, it becomes longer or bigger as well as thinner, usually because it is pulled.

frown^{복습}
[fraun]

n. 찌푸린 얼굴; v. 얼굴을 찡그리다, 눈살을 찌푸리다
A frown is a look that your face makes with your eyebrows drawn together because you are annoyed or puzzled.

Check Your Reading Speed

1분에 몇 단어를 읽는지 리딩 속도를 측정해보세요.

$$\frac{457 \text{ words}}{\text{reading time } (\quad) \text{ sec}} \times 60 = (\quad) \text{ WPM}$$

Build Your Vocabulary

bite^{복습}
[bait]

v. (bit–bit) 물다, 물어뜯다; n. 물기; 한 입(의 분량)
If you bite your lip or your tongue, you stop yourself from saying something that you want to say, because it would be the wrong thing to say in the circumstances.

whisper^{복습}
[hwíspər]

v. 속삭이다
When you whisper, you say something very quietly.

lag^{복습}
[læg]

v. 뒤에 처지다, 뒤떨어지다
If one thing or person lags behind another thing or person, their progress is slower than that of the other.

stammer*
[stǽmər]

v. 말을 더듬다, 더듬으며 말하다
If you stammer, you speak with difficulty, hesitating and repeating words or sounds.

bother^{복습}
[báðər]

v. 귀찮게 하다, 괴롭히다; 일부러 ~하다, 애를 쓰다
If someone bothers you, they talk to you when you want to be left alone or interrupt you when you are busy.

snap^{복습}
[snæp]

v. (화난 목소리로) 딱딱거리다; 딱[툭] (하고) 부러뜨리다, 부러지다
If someone snaps at you, they speak to you in a sharp, unfriendly way.

explode*
[iksplóud]

v. 폭발하다, 격발하다; 폭발시키다
If someone explodes, they express strong feelings suddenly and violently.

slam^{복습}
[slæm]

v. 털썩 내려놓다; (문을) 탕 닫다, 세게 치다; n. 쾅 (하는 소리)
If you slam something down, you put it there quickly and with great force.

sidewalk^{복습}
[sáidwɔːk]

n. (포장한) 보도, 인도
A sidewalk is a path with a hard surface by the side of a road.

hysterical^{복습}
[histérikəl]

a. 히스테리 상태의, 발작적인 (hysterically ad. 흥분하여)
Hysterical laughter is loud and uncontrolled.

fist^{복습}
[fist]

n. (쥔) 주먹
Your hand is referred to as your fist when you have bent your fingers in toward the palm in order to hit someone, to make an angry gesture, or to hold something.

shriek*
[ʃriːk]

v. 새된 소리를 지르다, 비명을 지르다; n. 비명
When someone shrieks, they make a short, very loud cry, for example because they are suddenly surprised, are in pain, or are laughing.

86

anticipate[*]
[æntísəpèit]

v. 예상하나, 미리 고려하나; 기대하나 (anticipation n. 예상, 예측)
If you anticipate an event, you realize in advance that it may happen and you are prepared for it.

tap 복습
[tæp]

① v. 가볍게 두드리다; n. 가볍게 두드리기 ② n. 주둥이, (수도 등의) 꼭지
If you tap something, you hit it with a quick light blow or a series of quick light blows.

slug 복습
[slʌg]

v. (주먹으로) 세게 때리다, 강타하다
If you slug someone, you hit them hard.

stomach 복습
[stʌ́mək]

n. 배, 복부; 위
You can refer to the front part of your body below your waist as your stomach.

bend[**]
[bend]

v. (bent–bent) 구부리다, 굽히다, 숙이다; n. 커브, 굽음
When you bend, you move the top part of your body downward and forward.

flail
[fleil]

v. 휘두르다; 도리깨질하다; n. 도리깨
If your arms or legs flail or if you flail them about, they wave about in an energetic but uncontrolled way.

defend[*]
[difénd]

v. 방어하다, 지키다
If you defend someone or something, you take action in order to protect them.

punch 복습
[pʌntʃ]

v. 주먹으로 치다, 때리다; n. 주먹으로 한 대 침, 펀치
If you punch someone or something, you hit them hard with your fist.

flat[***]
[flæt]

a. 평평한, 납작해진; n. 평평한 부분
Something that is flat is level, smooth, or even, rather than sloping, curved, or uneven.

kneel[*]
[ni:l]

v. (knelt–knelt) 무릎 꿇다
When you kneel, you bend your legs so that your knees are touching the ground.

slap[*]
[slæp]

v. 찰싹 때리다; 털썩 놓다; n. 찰싹 (때림)
If you slap someone, you hit them with the palm of your hand.

count 복습
[kaunt]

v. 수를 세다, 계산하다; 중요하다; (정식으로) 인정되다; n. 셈, 계산
When you count, you say all the numbers one after another up to a particular number.

bellow
[bélou]

v. (우렁찬 소리로) 고함치다
If someone bellows, they shout angrily in a loud, deep voice.

marvelous[*]
[máːrvələs]

a. 놀라운, 훌륭한
If you describe someone or something as marvelous, you are emphasizing that they are very good.

clap[*]
[klæp]

v. 박수를 치다; n. 박수
When you clap, you hit your hands together to show appreciation or attract attention.

1. What did Bradley think would happen if he tried being good?
   A. He thought that his grades would get better.
   B. He thought that Jeff would be his friend again.
   C. He thought that Colleen would invite him to her party.
   D. He thought that people would know he wasn't a monster.

2. Why did Bradley put on mismatched socks?
   A. He was too excited and hadn't realized what he did.
   B. He couldn't find a matched pair of socks.
   C. He wanted to show Carla.
   D. Those were his only clean socks.

3. Why was Bradley disappointed in the girls' bathroom?
   A. Nobody was in there.
   B. It looked like the boys' bathroom.
   C. The water wasn't running in the sinks.
   D. It smelled better than the boys' bathroom.

4. Why had Bradley not been allowed to check out books from the library?
   A. He used to scribble in them and rip them up.
   B. His grades hadn't been good enough.
   C. He didn't have a library card.
   D. His mother hadn't signed a form.

5. How did Carla feel about mismatched socks?
   A. She hated them and never wore them.
   B. She liked them and wore them, too.
   C. She thought that it was for children.
   D. She thought they looked silly.

6. Why did Bradley decide to do his homework?
   A. He wanted to go to a good college.
   B. He wanted to get a gold star.
   C. He was doing it for Carla.
   D. He wanted to be like Jeff.

7. Who did NOT help Bradley with his arithmetic homework?
   A. His father
   B. His mother
   C. Claudia
   D. Jeff

1분에 몇 단어를 읽는지 리딩 속도를 측정해보세요.

$$\frac{901 \text{ words}}{\text{reading time (\quad) sec}} \times 60 = (\qquad) \text{ WPM}$$

Build Your Vocabulary

sock*
[sak]

n. 양말
Socks are pieces of clothing which cover your foot and ankle and are worn inside shoes.

tie**
[tai]

v. 매다, 끈을 묶다; n. 넥타이
If you tie a piece of string or cloth around something or tie something with a piece of string or cloth, you put the piece of string or cloth around it and fasten the ends together.

shoelace
[ʃúːlèis]

n. 신발끈, 구두끈
Shoelaces are long, narrow pieces of material like pieces of string that you use to fasten your shoes.

fade*
[feid]

v. (색이) 바래다; 희미해지다; 시들다
When a colored object fades or when the light fades it, it gradually becomes paler.

complain**
[kəmpléin]

v. 불평하다, 투덜거리다
If you complain about a situation, you say that you are not satisfied with it.

serve***
[səːrv]

v. (음식을) 제공하다; 일하다, 복무하다; n. (테니스 등의) 서브
When you serve food and drink, you give people food and drink.

lumpy
[lʌ́mpi]

a. 덩어리가 많은
Something that is lumpy contains lumps or is covered with lumps.

spoonful*
[spúːnfùl]

n. 한 숟가락 가득(한 분량)
You can refer to an amount of food resting on a spoon as a spoonful of food.

swallow복습
[swálou]

v. 삼키다, 목구멍으로 넘기다; (초조해서) 마른침을 삼키다
If you swallow something, you cause it to go from your mouth down into your stomach.

glop
[glap]

n. (기분 나쁘게) 질척거리는 것
Glop is unappetizing food, especially of a semiliquid consistency.

withdraw*
[wiðdrɔ́ː]

v. (withdrew–withdrawn) 빼내다; 철회하다, 물러나다
If you withdraw something from a place, you remove it or take it away.

elbow복습
[élbou]

n. 팔꿈치; v. 팔꿈치로 쿡 찌르다
Your elbow is the part of your arm where the upper and lower halves of the arm are joined.

bump[*]
[bʌmp]

v. (쾅 히고) 부딪치다, 충돌하다; n. 충돌; 혹
If you bump into something or someone, you accidentally hit them while you are moving.

glare^{복습}
[glɛər]

v. 노려보다; 번쩍번쩍 빛나다; n. 노려봄; 섬광
If you glare at someone, you look at them with an angry expression on your face.

puzzle[*]
[pʌzl]

v. 곤혹스럽게 하다, 난처하게 하다; n. 수수께끼, 어려운 문제
If something puzzles you, you do not understand it and feel confused.

spill^{복습}
[spil]

v. 엎지르다, 흘리다; n. 엎지름, 유출
If a liquid spills or if you spill it, it accidentally flows over the edge of a container.

on purpose^{복습}

idiom 고의로, 일부러
If you do something on purpose, you do it intentionally.

mess^{복습}
[mes]

n. 엉망진창, 난잡함; v. 망쳐놓다, 방해하다
If you say that something is a mess or in a mess, you think that it is in an untidy state.

burst^{**}
[bə:rst]

v. 갑자기 ~하다, 터지다, 파열하다; n. 폭발, 파열; 돌발
If you burst out doing something, you begin doing it suddenly.

demand^{복습}
[dimǽnd]

v. 묻다, 요구하다, 청구하다; n. 요구, 수요
If you demand something such as information or action, you ask for it in a very forceful way.

appreciate^{복습}
[əprí:ʃièit]

v. 고맙게 생각하다; 평가하다, 감상하다
If you appreciate something that someone has done for you or is going to do for you, you are grateful for it.

stare^{복습}
[stɛər]

v. 응시하다, 뚫어지게 보다
If you stare at someone or something, you look at them for a long time.

edge^{복습}
[edʒ]

n. 가장자리, 변두리, 끝; v. 조금씩[살살] 움직이다; 테두리를 두르다
The edge of something is the place or line where it stops, or the part of it that is furthest from the middle.

sneaker
[sní:kər]

n. (pl.) 고무창 운동화
Sneakers are casual shoes with rubber soles.

punch^{복습}
[pʌntʃ]

v. 주먹으로 치다, 때리다; n. 주먹으로 한 대 침, 펀치
If you punch someone or something, you hit them hard with your fist.

attention^{**}
[əténʃən]

n. 주의, 관심; 배려; 차렷의 자세
If you pay attention to someone, you watch them, listen to them, or take notice of them.

determined[*]
[ditə́:rmind]

a. 결연한, 굳게 결심한
If you are determined to do something, you have made a firm decision to do it and will not let anything stop you.

fold^{복습}
[fould]

v. (손 · 팔 · 다리를) 끼다, 포개다; 접다, 접어 포개다
If you fold your arms or hands, you bring them together and cross or link them, for example over your chest.

hold back

idiom 자제하다; 감추다
If you hold back something like tears or laughter, you stop yourself from expressing or showing how you feel.

glance^{복습}
[glæns]

v. 흘긋 보다, 잠깐 보다; n. 흘긋 봄
If you glance at something or someone, you look at them very quickly and then look away again immediately.

out of the corner of one's eye

idiom 곁눈질로, 슬쩍
If you see something out of the corner of your eye, you look at it at the edge of your vision.

snarl*
[snɑːrl]

v. 으르렁거리다, 으르렁거리듯 말하다; n. 으르렁거림
If you snarl something, you say it in a fierce, angry way.

twin*
[twin]

n. 쌍둥이 중의 하나; a. 쌍둥이의, 한 쌍의
If two people are twins, they have the same mother and were born on the same day.

exclaim^{복습}
[ikskléim]

v. 외치다, 소리치다
If you exclaim, you say or shout something suddenly because of surprise, fear and pleasure.

recess^{복습}
[ríːses]

n. (학교의) 쉬는 시간; 휴회
A recess is a short period of time when you have a rest or a change from what you are doing, especially if you are working or if you are in a boring or unpleasant situation.

stumble^{복습}
[stʌmbl]

v. 비틀거리며 걷다, 발부리가 걸리다; n. 비틀거림
If you stumble, you put your foot down awkwardly while you are walking or running and nearly fall over.

surround^{복습}
[səráund]

v. 둘러싸다, 에워싸다; n. 둘러싸는 것; 환경, 주위
If a person or thing is surrounded by something, that thing is situated all around them.

grocery*
[gróusəri]

n. (pl.) 식료 잡화류; 식료 잡화점
Groceries are foods you buy at a grocer's or at a supermarket such as flour, sugar, and tinned foods.

dash^{복습}
[dæʃ]

v. 돌진하다; 내던지다; n. 돌격; 소량
If you dash somewhere, you run or go there quickly and suddenly.

chase^{복습}
[ʧeis]

v. 뒤쫓다; 추구하다; 쫓아내다; n. 추적, 추격
If you chase someone, or chase after them, you run after them or follow them quickly in order to catch or reach them.

smash*
[smæʃ]

v. 세게 충돌하다; 때려 부수다, 깨뜨리다; n. 강타; 부서지는 소리; 분쇄
If you smash into someone or something, you hit them or it very hard, causing damage.

wail
[weil]

v. (큰소리로) 울부짖다, 통곡하다; n. 울부짖음, 비탄
If someone wails, they make long, loud, high-pitched cries which express sorrow or pain.

helpless*
[hélplis]

a. 무력한, 속수무책의 (helplessly ad. 무력하게, 어쩔 수 없이)
If you are helpless, you do not have the strength or power to do anything useful or to control or protect yourself.

concrete[*]
[kánkriːt]

n. 콘크리트; a. 유형이, 구체적인
Concrete is a substance used for building which is made by mixing together cement, sand, small stones, and water.

auditorium^{복습}
[ɔ̀ːditɔ́ːriəm]

n. 강당, 회관; 청중석, 관객석
An auditorium is a large room, hall, or building which is used for events such as meetings and concerts.

mutter^{복습}
[mʌ́tər]

v. 중얼거리다, 불평하다; n. 중얼거림, 불평
If you mutter, you speak very quietly so that you cannot easily be heard, often because you are complaining about something.

lean^{복습}
[liːn]

v. ~을 ~에 기대 놓다 기울다, 기울이다, (몸을) 숙이다; ~에 기대다
If you lean an object on or against something, you place the object so that it is partly supported by that thing.

prop
[prap]

v. 받치다, 기대 세우다, 버티다; n. 지주, 버팀목
If you prop an object on or against something, you support it by putting something underneath it or by resting it somewhere.

Check Your Reading Speed

1분에 몇 단어를 읽는지 리딩 속도를 측정해보세요.

$$\frac{676 \text{ words}}{\text{reading time ( ) sec}} \times 60 = (\qquad) \text{ WPM}$$

Build Your Vocabulary

knock^{복습}
[nak]

v. 치다, 부수다; (문을) 두드리다, 노크하다; n. 노크; 타격
(knock someone over idiom ~을 때려눕히다)
If you knock someone over, you hit them, making them fall down.

beat^{복습}
[bi:t]

v. (beat–beat) 치다, 두드리다; 패배시키다, 이기다; (심장이) 고동치다;
n. [음악] 박자, 고동
If you beat someone or something, you hit them very hard.

concentrate**
[kánsəntrèit]

v. 집중하다, 전념하다
If you concentrate on something, you give all your attention to it.

cheer^{복습}
[ʧiər]

v. 환호성을 지르다, 응원하다; n. 환호(성)
When people cheer, they shout loudly to show their approval or to encourage someone who is doing something such as taking part in a game.

gang^{복습}
[gæŋ]

n. 패거리, 한 때, 무리
A gang is a group of people who go around together and often deliberately cause trouble.

sack^{복습}
[sæk]

n. (쇼핑 물건을 담는 크고 튼튼한 종이) 봉지; 부대, 자루; v. 자루에 넣다
Sacks are used to carry or store things such as vegetables or coal.

yell^{복습}
[jel]

v. 소리치다, 고함치다; n. 고함소리, 부르짖음
If you yell, you shout loudly, usually because you are excited, angry, or in pain.

budge
[bʌdʒ]

v. 약간 움직이다, 꿈쩍하다
If something will not budge or you cannot budge it, it will not move.

desperate**
[déspərət]

a. 필사적인; 자포자기의, 절망적인
If you are desperate for something or desperate to do something, you want or need it very much indeed.

stick^{복습}
[stik]

① v. 찔러 넣다, 찌르다; 내밀다; 붙이다, 달라붙다 ② n. 막대기, 지팡이
If you stick something somewhere, you put it there in a rather casual way.

toilet^{복습}
[tɔ́ilit]

n. 변기; 화장실
A toilet is a large bowl with a seat, or a platform with a hole, which is connected to a water system and which you use when you want to get rid of urine or feces from your body.

sink^{복습}
[siŋk]

n. 세면대; (부엌의) 싱크대, 개수대; v. 가라앉다, 빠지다
A sink is a large bowl, usually with taps for hot and cold water, for washing your hands and face.

94

dispenser
[dispénsər]

n. (손잡이 · 단추 등을 눌러 안에 든 것을 바로 뽑아 쓸 수 있는) 기계, 용기
A dispenser is a machine or container designed so that you can get an item or quantity of something from it in an easy and convenient way.

separate**
[sépərèit]

a. 개개의, 개별적인; v. 가르다, 떼다, 분리하다
If you refer to separate things, you mean several different things, rather than just one thing.

stall*
[stɔ:l]

n. 칸막이한 작은 방; 노점; 마구간
A stall is a small enclosed area in a room which is used for a particular purpose, for example a shower.

risk^{복습}
[risk]

v. ~의 위험을 무릅쓰다; (~을) 위태롭게 하다; n. 위험
If you risk doing something, you do it, even though you know that it might have undesirable consequences.

roast*
[roust]

v. 굽다, 불에 쬐다; (고기가) 구워지다 (roast beef n. 소고기 구이)
When you roast meat or other food, you cook it by dry heat in an oven or over a fire.

hop^{복습}
[hap]

v. 깡충 뛰다, 뛰어오르다; n. 깡충깡충 뜀
If you hop, you move along by jumping.

private**
[práivət]

a. 공개하지 않는, 비밀의; 사적인, 개인의
You can use private to describe situations or activities that are understood only by the people involved in them, and not by anyone else.

flush*
[flʌʃ]

v. (물이) 왈칵 흘러나오다; (얼굴 등을) 붉히다; n. (볼 등의) 홍조
When someone flushes a toilet after using it, they fill the toilet bowl with water in order to clean it, usually by pressing a handle or pulling a chain. You can also say that a toilet flushes.

zip*
[zip]

v. 지퍼로 잠그다, 지퍼로 열다; n. 지퍼
When you zip something, you fasten it using a zip.

exhale
[ekshéil]

v. (숨 · 연기 등을) 내쉬다, 내뿜다
When you exhale, you breathe out the air that is in your lungs.

freeze^{복습}
[fri:z]

v. (froze–frozen) 얼다, 얼리다; n. (임금 · 가격 등의) 동결
If someone who is moving freezes, they suddenly stop and become completely still and quiet.

dart^{복습}
[da:rt]

v. 돌진하다; (시선 · 화살 · 빛 등을) 던지다, 쏘다; n. 던지는 화살, 다트
If a person or animal darts somewhere, they move there suddenly and quickly.

round^{복습}
[raund]

v. (모퉁이 · 커브 등을) 돌다; 둥글게 만들다; a. 둥근, 동그란, 원형의
If you round a place or obstacle, you move in a curve past the edge or corner of it.

pound*
[paund]

① v. 쿵쿵 울리다, 마구 치다, 세게 두드리다; n. 타격 ② n. 파운드(무게의 단위) ③ n. 울타리, 우리
If you pound something or pound on it, you hit it with great force, usually loudly and repeatedly.

1분에 몇 단어를 읽는지 리딩 속도를 측정해보세요.

$$\frac{903 \text{ words}}{\text{reading time (\quad) sec}} \times 60 = (\qquad) \text{ WPM}$$

Build Your Vocabulary

sleeve^{복습}
[sliːv]

n. (옷의) 소매, 소맷자락 (sleeveless a. 소매 없는)
The sleeves of a coat, shirt, or other item of clothing are the parts that cover your arms.

checker
[ʧékər]

n. 바둑판[체크]무늬; 계산대 직원 (checkered a. 바둑판무늬의)
Something that is checkered has a pattern with squares of two or more different colors.

slam^{복습}
[slæm]

v. 세게 치다, (문을) 탕 닫다; 털썩 내려놓다; n. 쾅 (하는 소리)
If one thing slams into or against another, it crashes into it with great force.

fist^{복습}
[fist]

n. (쥔) 주먹
Your hand is referred to as your fist when you have bent your fingers in toward the palm in order to hit someone, to make an angry gesture, or to hold something.

toilet^{복습}
[tɔ́ilit]

n. 변기; 화장실
A toilet is a large bowl with a seat, or a platform with a hole, which is connected to a water system and which you use when you want to get rid of urine or feces from your body.

considerate[*]
[kənsídərət]

a. 사려 깊은, 동정심 많은
Someone who is considerate pays attention to the needs, wishes, or feelings of other people.

shrug^{복습}
[ʃrʌg]

v. (양 손바닥을 내보이면서 어깨를) 으쓱하다; n. 으쓱하기
If you shrug, you raise your shoulders to show that you are not interested in something or that you do not know or care about something.

carton[*]
[kaːrtn]

n. (음식이나 음료를 담는) 곽, 통; 상자
A carton is a plastic or cardboard container in which food or drink is sold.

plate^{복습}
[pleit]

n. 접시, 그릇
A plate is a round or oval flat dish that is used to hold food.

slice[*]
[slais]

v. 자르다, 썰다, 얇게 베다; n. 얇게 썬 조각, 한 조각
To slice something means to cut them easily with one movement of a sharp knife or edge.

cucumber
[kjúːkʌmbər]

n. 오이
A cucumber is a long thin vegetable with a hard green skin and wet transparent flesh.

96

trade***
[treid]

v. 교환하다; 장사하다; n. 교환, 무역
If someone trades one thing for another or if two people trade things, they agree to exchange one thing for the other thing.

bite^{복습}
[bait]

n. 한 입(의 분량); 물기; v. 물다, 물어뜯다
A bite is the amount of food you take into your mouth when you bite it.

roast^{복습}
[roust]

v. 굽다, 불에 쬐다; (고기가) 구워지다 (roast beef n. 소고기 구이)
When you roast meat or other food, you cook it by dry heat in an oven or over a fire.

chase^{복습}
[ʧeis]

v. 뒤쫓다; 추구하다; 쫓아내다; n. 추적, 추격
If you chase someone, or chase after them, you run after them or follow them quickly in order to catch or reach them.

tie^{복습}
[tai]

v. 매다, 끈을 묶다; n. 넥타이
If you tie two things together or tie them, you fasten them together with a knot.

spoonful^{복습}
[spúːnfùl]

n. 한 숟가락 가득(한 분량)
You can refer to an amount of food resting on a spoon as a spoonful of food.

amaze^{복습}
[əméiz]

v. 깜짝 놀라게 하다 (amazing a. 놀랄 만한)
If something amazes you, it surprises you very much.

nod^{복습}
[nad]

v. 끄덕이다, 끄덕여 표시하다; n. (동의 · 인사 · 신호 · 명령의) 끄덕임
If you nod, you move your head downward and upward to show agreement, understanding, or approval.

straw^{복습}
[strɔː]

n. 빨대; 지푸라기, 짚
A straw is a thin tube of paper or plastic, which you use to suck a drink into your mouth.

practically*
[præktikəli]

ad. 거의, ~이나 다름없이; 실지로, 사실상
Practically means almost, but not completely or exactly.

run out of

idiom ~을 다 써버리다, 동나다, 다 하다
If a person or a machine runs out of a supply of something, they finish it or use it all up.

check out^{복습}

idiom (책 등을) 빌리다, 대출하다
If you check something out, you borrow it such as a book or a video from a library.

scribble^{복습}
[skribl]

v. 낙서하다; 갈겨쓰다, 휘갈기다; n. 낙서
To scribble means to make meaningless marks or rough drawings using a pencil or pen.

rip^{복습}
[rip]

v. 찢다, 벗겨내다; n. 찢어진 틈, 잡아 찢음
When something rips or when you rip it, you tear it forcefully with your hands or with a tool such as a knife.

ruin**
[ruːin]

v. 망치다, 못쓰게 만들다; 몰락하다; n. 파멸, 멸망
To ruin something means to severely harm, damage, or spoil it.

spit^{복습}
[spit]

v. (spit-spit) (침 등을) 뱉다; 내뱉듯이 말하다; n. 침
If you spit liquid or food somewhere, you force a small amount of it out of your mouth.

sock^{복습}
[sak]

n. 양말
Socks are pieces of clothing which cover your foot and ankle and are worn inside shoes.

match**
[mætʃ]

v. 조화하다, 어울리다; 필적하다, 대등하다; n. 상대, 경기
(mismatched a. 어울리지 않는)
If something of a particular color or design matches another thing, they have the same color or design, or have a pleasing appearance when they are used together.

befuddle
[bifʌdl]

v. 어리둥절하게 하다; 정신을 잃게 하다 (befuddled a. 당혹스러운)
If something befuddles you, it confuses your mind or thoughts.

twist^{복습}
[twist]

v. 비틀다, 돌리다, 꼬다; n. 뒤틀림; 엉킴 (twisted a. 비뚤어진)
If you twist something, especially a part of your body, or if it twists, it moves into an unusual, uncomfortable, or bent position, for example because of being hit or pushed, or because you are upset.

genuine*
[dʒénjuin]

a. 진실한, 진심 어린; 진짜의, 진품의
Genuine refers to things such as emotions that are real and not pretended.

tear^{복습}
[tiə:r]

① n. 눈물 ② v. 부리나케 가다; 찢다, 찢어지다; n. 찢음
Tears are the drops of salty liquid that come out of your eyes when you are crying.

confidence^{복습}
[kánfədəns]

n. 신용, 신뢰; 자신(감), 확신
If you have confidence in someone, you feel that you can trust them.

crack^{복습}
[kræk]

v. 갑자기 날카로운 소리를 내다; 금이 가다, 깨다; n. 갈라진 금
If your voice cracks when you are speaking or singing, it changes in pitch because you are feeling a strong emotion.

make a big deal out of

idiom ~을 과장하여 생각하다
If someone makes a big deal out of something, they become angry about it and complain or treat it as if it were very important.

sob^{복습}
[sab]

v. 흐느껴 울다; n. 흐느낌, 오열
When someone sobs, they cry in a noisy way, breathing in short breaths.

wipe^{복습}
[waip]

v. 닦다, 닦아 내다; n. 닦기
If you wipe something, you rub its surface to remove dirt or liquid from it.

sniffle
[snifl]

v. 코를 훌쩍이다, 코를 훌쩍거리며 말하다; n. 코를 훌쩍거림
If you sniffle, you keep sniffing, usually because you are crying or have a cold.

whisper^{복습}
[hwíspər]

v. 속삭이다
When you whisper, you say something very quietly.

glisten
[glisn]

v. 반짝이다, 반짝반짝 빛나다; n. 반짝임
If something glistens, it shines, usually because it is wet or oily.

check**
[tʃiːk]

n. 뺨, 볼

Your cheeks are the sides of your face below your eyes.

1분에 몇 단어를 읽는지 리딩 속도를 측정해보세요.

$$\frac{1{,}373 \text{ words}}{\text{reading time (} \quad \text{) sec}} \times 60 = (\quad) \text{ WPM}$$

Build Your Vocabulary

stomach^{복습}
[stʌ́mək]

n. 배, 복부; 위
You can refer to the front part of your body below your waist as your stomach.

chew^{복습}
[ʧuː]

v. 씹다, 씹어서 으깨다
If a person or animal chews an object, they bite it with their teeth.

hopeless^{복습}
[hóuplis]

a. 가망 없는, 절망적인 (hopelessly ad. 절망하여)
Someone or something thing that is hopeless is certain to fail or be unsuccessful.

arithmetic*
[əríθmətik]

n. 산수, 셈
Arithmetic is the part of mathematics that is concerned with the addition, subtraction, multiplication, and division of numbers.

mess^{복습}
[mes]

n. 엉망진창, 난잡함; v. 망쳐놓다, 방해하다 (messy a. 지저분한, 엉망인)
If you say that something is a mess or in a mess, you think that it is in an untidy state.

dull**
[dʌl]

a. 무딘, 뾰족하지 않은; 둔한
If a knife or blade is dull, it is not sharp.

bully^{복습}
[búli]

n. 약자를 괴롭히는 사람; v. 곯리다, 겁주다
A bully is someone who uses their strength or power to hurt or frighten other people.

eye^{복습}
[ai]

v. (탐이 나거나 의심스러워) 쳐다보다; n. 눈
If you eye someone or something in a particular way, you look at them carefully in that way.

suspicious^{복습}
[səspíʃəs]

a. 의심하는, 수상쩍은 (suspiciously ad. 의심스러운 듯이)
If you are suspicious of someone or something, you do not trust them, and are careful when dealing with them.

figure out

idiom ~을 생각해내다, 발견하다; 계산하다
If you figure out a solution to a problem or the reason for something, you succeed in solving it or understanding it.

reluctant^{복습}
[rilʌ́ktənt]

a. 꺼리는, 마지못해 하는, 주저하는 (reluctantly ad. 마지못해서, 꺼려하여)
If you are reluctant to do something, you are unwilling to do it and hesitate before doing it, or do it slowly and without enthusiasm.

sneaker^{복습}
[sníːkər]

n. (pl.) 고무창 운동화
Sneakers are casual shoes with rubber soles.

sigh ^{복습}
[sai]

v. 한숨 쉬다; n. 한숨, 탄식
When you sigh, you let out a deep breath, as a way of expressing feelings such as disappointment, tiredness, or pleasure.

wander ^{복습}
[wándər]

v. 돌아다니다, 방황하다; n. 유랑, 방랑
If your mind wanders or your thoughts wander, you stop concentrating on something and start thinking about other things.

concentrate ^{복습}
[kánsəntrèit]

v. 집중하다, 전념하다
If you concentrate on something, you give all your attention to it.

exclaim ^{복습}
[ikskléim]

v. 외치다, 소리치다
If you exclaim, you say or shout something suddenly because of surprise, fear and pleasure.

divide***
[diváid]

v. 나누다, 분할하다
If you divide a larger number by a smaller number or divide a smaller number into a larger number, you calculate how many times the smaller number can fit exactly into the larger number.

multiply**
[mʌ́ltiplai]

v. 곱하다; 늘리다, 증가하다
If you multiply one number by another, you add the first number to itself as many times as is indicated by the second number.

donkey ^{복습}
[dánki]

n. [동물] 당나귀
A donkey is an animal which is like a horse but which is smaller and has longer ears.

reverse*
[rivə́:rs]

v. (정반대로) 뒤바꾸다, 반전시키다; n. (정)반대
If you reverse the order of a set of things, you arrange them in the opposite order, so that the first thing comes last.

inverse
[invə́:rs]

v. 거꾸로 하다, 반대로 하다; a. 정반대의, 반비례의
If you inverse something, you change it to its opposite.

multiplication*
[mʌ̀ltəplikéiʃən]

n. 곱셈; 증가, 증대
Multiplication is the process of calculating the total of one number multiplied by another.

addition**
[ədíʃən]

n. 덧셈; 추가, 부가
Addition is the process of calculating the total of two or more numbers.

cancel**
[kǽnsəl]

v. [수학] 약분하다, 상쇄하다; 지우다, 취소하다; n. 취소, 삭제
If two or more things cancel out or one cancels out the other, they are equally important, but have an opposite effect on a situation so that the situation does not change.

erase ^{복습}
[iréis]

v. (지우개 등으로) 지우다; (완전히) 지우다, 없애다
If you erase something such as writing or a mark, you remove it, usually by rubbing it with an eraser.

smudge
[smʌdʒ]

n. 얼룩, 더러움; v. 더럽히다, 얼룩지다
A smudge is a dirty mark.

fraction*
[frǽkʃən]

n. [수학] 분수; 파편, 단편, 조금, 소량
A fraction is a number that can be expressed as a proportion of two whole numbers. For example, 1/2 and 1/3 are both fractions.

end up

idiom (구어) 마침내는 (~으로) 되다, 끝나다
If you end up doing something or end up in a particular state, you do that thing or get into that state even though you did not originally intend to.

slam^{복습}
[slæm]

v. (문을) 탕 닫다, 세게 치다; 털썩 내려놓다; n. 쾅 (하는 소리)
If you slam a door or window or if it slams, it shuts noisily and with great force.

disgust^{복습}
[disgʌ́st]

n. 싫음, 혐오감; v. 역겹게 하다, 넌더리나게 하다
Disgust is a feeling of very strong dislike or disapproval.

puzzle^{복습}
[pʌzl]

n. 수수께끼, 어려운 문제; v. 곤혹스럽게 하다, 난처하게 하다
(crossword puzzle n. 십자말풀이)
A puzzle is a question, game, or toy which you have to think about carefully in order to answer it correctly or put it together properly.

plop
[plap]

v. 털썩 주저앉다; 퐁당[툭] 하고 떨어지다; n. 퐁당 (하는 소리)
If something plops somewhere, it drops there with a soft, gentle sound.

inquisitive
[inkwízətiv]

a. 호기심이 많은, 알고 싶어 하는 (inquisitively ad. 몹시 알고 싶어 하여)
An inquisitive person likes finding out about things, especially secret things.

complain^{복습}
[kəmpléin]

v. 불평하다, 투덜거리다
If you complain about a situation, you say that you are not satisfied with it.

delight^{복습}
[diláit]

v. 즐겁게 하다, 매우 기쁘게 하다; n. 기쁨, 즐거움 (delighted a. 즐거워하는)
If something delights you, it gives you a lot of pleasure.

neat^{복습}
[ni:t]

a. 말끔한, 깔끔한; 멋진, 훌륭한
A neat place, thing, or person is tidy and smart, and has everything in the correct place.

sheet^{복습}
[ʃi:t]

n. (종이) 한 장; (침대) 시트
A sheet of paper is a rectangular piece of paper.

disbelief^{복습}
[dìsbilí:f]

n. 믿기지 않음, 불신감
Disbelief is not believing that something is true or real.

allow^{복습}
[əláu]

v. 허락하다, ~하게 두다; 인정하다
If someone is allowed to do something, it is all right for them to do it and they will not get into trouble.

scare^{복습}
[skɛər]

v. 위협하다, 겁나게 하다 (scared a. 무서워하는, 겁먹은)
If something scares you, it frightens or worries you.

drawer**
[drɔːr]

n. 서랍
A drawer is part of a desk, chest, or other piece of furniture that is shaped like a box and is designed for putting things in.

equation*
[ikwéiʒən]

n. 등식, 방정식
An equation is a mathematical statement saying that two amounts or values are the same.

abrupt[*]
[əbrʌ́pt]

a. 갑작스러운, 뜻밖의; 퉁명스러운 (abruptly ad. 갑지기)

An abrupt change or action is very sudden, often in a way which is unpleasant.

glare[복습]
[glɛər]

v. 노려보다; 번쩍번쩍 빛나다; n. 노려봄; 섬광

If you glare at someone, you look at them with an angry expression on your face.

patient[**]
[péiʃənt]

a. 인내심 있는, 참을성 있는; n. 환자 (patiently ad. 참을성 있게, 끈기 있게)

If you are patient, you stay calm and do not get annoyed, for example when something takes a long time, or when someone is not doing what you want them to do.

separate[복습]
[sépərèit]

a. 개개의, 개별적인; v. 가르다, 떼다, 분리하다 (separately ad. 따로따로)

If you refer to separate things, you mean several different things, rather than just one thing.

reduce[**]
[ridjúːs]

v. [수학] 약분하다; (규모 · 크기 · 양 등을) 줄이다

In mathematics to reduce means to modify or simplify the form of an expression or equation, especially by substitution of one term by another.

chapters 29 to 32

1. What did Bradley do when he went to turn in his homework?
   A. He tore it in half and dropped it in the waste basket.
   B. He put it on the pile of homework from other students.
   C. He folded it neatly and put it in his desk.
   D. He decided to bring it to Carla instead.

2. What did Carla say was the main thing about homework?
   A. Doing it and getting a good grade
   B. Doing it and getting a gold star
   C. Doing it and learning something
   D. Doing it with neat handwriting

3. Why did Bradley borrow a book from Carla?
   A. He wanted to practice reading.
   B. He had a book report due the next week.
   C. Carla had talked about the book earlier.
   D. Bradley wanted something to do instead of math.

4. Why did Mrs. Chalkers decide not to go to the meeting about Carla?
   A. She wanted Carla to get fired.
   B. She was busy during that time.
   C. She didn't like Carla very much.
   D. She didn't have any complaints.

5. What did Bradley do while Mrs. Ebbel taught arithmetic?
   A. He worked on his homework.
   B. He scribbled all over his desk.
   C. He paid close attention to her.
   D. He read the book that Carla had given him.

6. How did Bradley feel about having Carla's book?
   A. He felt that it was too heavy to carry around.
   B. He felt like nothing could go wrong with it around.
   C. He felt like some of the other students might try to steal it.
   D. He felt that it was a boring book after all.

7. How did Bradley avoid a fight with Jeff and his friends at lunch?
   A. He said hello to Jeff.
   B. He said sorry to Jeff.
   C. He walked away.
   D. He hid in the bathroom.

1분에 몇 단어를 읽는지 리딩 속도를 측정해보세요.

$$\frac{713 \text{ words}}{\text{reading time (\quad) sec}} \times 60 = (\qquad) \text{ WPM}$$

Build Your Vocabulary

steal^{복습}
[sti:l]

v. 훔치다, 도둑질하다
If you steal something from someone, you take it away from them without their permission and without intending to return it.

fold^{복습}
[fould]

v. 접다, 접어 포개다; (손 · 팔 · 다리를) 끼다, 포개다
If you fold something such as a piece of paper or cloth, you bend it so that one part covers another part, often pressing the edge so that it stays in place.

arithmetic^{복습}
[əríθmətik]

n. 산수, 셈
Arithmetic is the part of mathematics that is concerned with the addition, subtraction, multiplication, and division of numbers.

exact***
[igzǽkt]

a. 정확한, 정밀한 (exactly ad. 정확하게, 꼭)
Exact means correct in every detail.

horror^{복습}
[hɔ́:rər]

n. 공포, 전율
Horror is a feeling of great shock, fear, and worry caused by something extremely unpleasant.

tremble^{복습}
[trembl]

v. 떨다, 떨리다
If you tremble, you shake slightly because you are frightened or cold.

pillow^{복습}
[pílou]

n. 베개
A pillow is a rectangular cushion which you rest your head on when you are in bed.

sidewalk^{복습}
[sáidwɔ:k]

n. (포장한) 보도, 인도
A sidewalk is a path with a hard surface by the side of a road.

puddle^{복습}
[pʌdl]

n. 웅덩이; 뒤범벅; v. 흙탕물을 휘젓다
A puddle is a small, shallow pool of liquid that has spread on the ground.

stare^{복습}
[stɛər]

v. 응시하다, 뚫어지게 보다
If you stare at someone or something, you look at them for a long time.

horrify
[hɔ́:rəfài]

v. 충격을 주다, 소름끼치게 하다 (horrified a. 겁에 질린, 충격 받은)
If someone is horrified, they feel shocked or disgusted, because of something that they have seen or heard.

keep on the lookout for^{복습}

idiom (~이 있는지) 세심히 살피다, 지켜보다
If you keep on the lookout for something or someone, you are searching for it or them.

gang^{복습}
[gæn]

n. 패거리, 한 떼, 무리
A gang is a group of people who go around together and often deliberately cause trouble.

sneak^{복습}
[sni:k]

v. 살금살금 가다, 몰래 가다
If you sneak somewhere, you go there very quietly on foot, trying to avoid being seen or heard.

row^{복습}
[rou]

① n. 열, 줄 ② v. 노를 젓다, 배를 젓다; n. 노 젓기
A row of things or people is a number of them arranged in a line.

sheet^{복습}
[ʃi:t]

n. (종이) 한 장; (침대) 시트
A sheet of paper is a rectangular piece of paper.

turn in

idiom 제출하다, 건네다
If you turn in something such as a piece of written work, you give it to the person who asked you to do it.

pile**
[pail]

n. 쌓아 올린 더미; 다수; v. 쌓아 올리다; 쌓이다
A pile of things is a mass of them that is high in the middle and has sloping sides.

snap^{복습}
[snæp]

v. (화난 목소리로) 딱딱거리다; 딱[툭] (하고) 부러뜨리다, 부러지다
If someone snaps at you, they speak to you in a sharp, unfriendly way.

count^{복습}
[kaunt]

v. (정식으로) 인정되다; 수를 세다, 계산하다; 중요하다; n. 셈, 계산
If something counts or is counted as a particular thing, it is regarded as being that thing, especially in particular circumstances or under particular rules.

fumble
[fʌmbl]

v. 손으로 더듬어 찾다; 우물우물 말하다
If you fumble for something or fumble with something, you try and reach for it or hold it in a clumsy way.

breathe^{복습}
[bri:ð]

v. 호흡하다, 숨을 쉬다
When people or animals breathe, they take air into their lungs and let it out again.

hardly^{복습}
[há:rdli]

ad. 거의 ~아니다, 전혀 ~않다
When you say you can hardly do something, you are emphasizing that it is very difficult for you to do it.

faint*
[feint]

v. 기절하다; a. 희미한, 어렴풋한
If you faint, you lose consciousness for a short time, especially because you are hungry, or because of pain, heat, or shock.

telescope*
[téləskòup]

n. 망원경
A telescope is a long instrument shaped like a tube. It has lenses inside it that make distant things seem larger and nearer when you look through it.

pound^{복습}
[paund]

① v. 쿵쿵 울리다, 마구 치다, 세게 두드리다; n. 타격 ② n. 파운드(무게의 단위)
③ n. 울타리, 우리
If your heart is pounding, it is beating with an unusually strong and fast rhythm, usually because you are afraid.

rattle*
[rǽtl]

v. 왈각달각 소리 나다, 덜걱덜걱 움직이다; n. 덜거덕거리는 소리
When something rattles or when you rattle it, it makes short sharp knocking sounds because it is being shaken or it keeps hitting against something hard.

explode^{복습}
[iksplóud]

v. 폭발하다, 격발하다; 폭발시키다
If an object such as a bomb explodes or if someone or something explodes it, it bursts loudly and with great force, often causing damage or injury.

wastepaper^{복습}
[wéistpèipər]

n. 휴지, 폐지 (wastepaper basket n. 휴지통)
A wastepaper basket is a container for rubbish, especially paper, which is usually placed on the floor in the corner of a room or next to a desk.

instant*
[ínstənt]

n. 즉시, 순간; a. 즉시의, 즉각적인 (instantly ad. 즉시, 즉각)
An instant is an extremely short period of time.

normal^{복습}
[nɔ́:rməl]

a. 보통의, 정상의, 평범한
Something that is normal is usual and ordinary, and is what people expect.

exhale^{복습}
[ekshéil]

v. (숨 · 연기 등을) 내쉬다, 내뿜다
When you exhale, you breathe out the air that is in your lungs.

relieve*
[rilíːv]

v. 안도하게 하다; (긴장 · 걱정 등을) 덜다 (relieved a. 안심한, 안도한)
If something relieves an unpleasant feeling or situation, it makes it less unpleasant or causes it to disappear completely.

gaze*
[geiz]

v. 응시하다, 뚫어지게 보다; n. 주시, 응시
If you gaze at someone or something, you look steadily at them for a long time, for example because you find them attractive or interesting, or because you are thinking about something else.

1분에 몇 단어를 읽는지 리딩 속도를 측정해보세요.

$$\frac{1{,}031 \text{ words}}{\text{reading time ( ) sec}} \times 60 = (\quad) \text{ WPM}$$

Build Your Vocabulary

recess^{복습}
[rí:ses]

n. (학교의) 쉬는 시간; 휴회
A recess is a short period of time when you have a rest or a change from what you are doing, especially if you are working or if you are in a boring or unpleasant situation.

sort***
[sɔ:rt]

v. 분류하다, 골라내다; n. 종류, 부류
If you sort things, you separate them into different classes, groups, or places, for example so that you can do different things with them.

timid^{복습}
[tímid]

a. 소심한, 자신이 없는 (timidly ad. 소심하게)
If you describe someone's attitudes or actions as timid, you are criticizing them for being too cautious or slow to act.

hall^{복습}
[hɔ:l]

n. (건물 안의) 복도; (건물 입구 안쪽의) 현관
A hall in a building is a long passage with doors into rooms on both sides of it.

counsel^{복습}
[káunsəl]

v. 상담을 하다; n. 조언, 충고 (counselor n. 지도교사, 상담사)
If you counsel people, you give them advice about their problems.

hook^{복습}
[huk]

n. 갈고리, 훅, 걸쇠; v. 갈고리로 걸다
A hook is a bent piece of metal or plastic that is used for catching or holding things, or for hanging things up.

knock^{복습}
[nak]

v. (문을) 두드리다, 노크하다; 치다, 부수다; n. 노크; 타격
If you knock on something such as a door or window, you hit it, usually several times, to attract someone's attention.

greet^{복습}
[gri:t]

v. 인사하다; 환영하다, 맞이하다
When you greet someone, you say 'Hello' or shake hands with them.

appreciate^{복습}
[əprí:ʃièit]

v. 고맙게 생각하다; 평가하다, 감상하다
If you appreciate something that someone has done for you or is going to do for you, you are grateful for it.

squiggle^{복습}
[skwigl]

n. 구불구불한 선; v. 휘갈겨 쓰다
A squiggle is a line that bends and curls in an irregular way.

mouse^{복습}
[maus]

n. (pl. mice) [동물] 쥐, 생쥐
A mouse is a small furry animal with a long tail.

beam^{복습}
[bi:m]

v. 활짝 웃다; 비추다; n. 환한 얼굴; 빛줄기; [건축] 들보, 기둥
If you say that someone is beaming, you mean that they have a big smile on their face because they are happy, pleased, or proud about something.

rip^{복습}
[rip]

v. 찢다, 벗겨내다; n. 찢어진 틈, 잡아 찢음
When something rips or when you rip it, you tear it forcefully with your hands or with a tool such as a knife.

shrug^{복습}
[ʃrʌg]

v. (양 손바닥을 내보이면서 어깨를) 으쓱하다; n. 으쓱하기
If you shrug, you raise your shoulders to show that you are not interested in something or that you do not know or care about something.

giggle^{복습}
[gigl]

v. 낄낄 웃다; n. 낄낄 웃음
If someone giggles, they laugh in a childlike way, because they are amused, nervous, or embarrassed.

baffle
[bæfl]

v. 당황하게 하다, 어리둥절하게 하다 (baffled a. 당혹스러운)
If something baffles you, you cannot understand it or explain it.

subtract[*]
[səbtrǽkt]

v. 빼다, 감하다 (subtraction n. 뺄셈)
If you subtract one number from another, you do a calculation in which you take it away from the other number. For example, if you subtract 3 from 5, you get 2.

assure^{복습}
[əʃúər]

v. 단언하다, 확신하다, 보증하다
If you assure someone that something is true or will happen, you tell them that it is definitely true or will definitely happen, often in order to make them less worried.

silly^{**}
[síli]

a. 어리석은, 바보 같은; n. 바보, 멍청이
If you say that someone or something is silly, you mean that they are foolish, childish, or ridiculous.

expert[*]
[ékspə:rt]

n. 전문가; a. 숙련된, 노련한
An expert is a person who is very skilled at doing something or who knows a lot about a particular subject.

due^{***}
[dju:]

a. ~하기로 되어 있는, ~할 예정인
If something is due at a particular time, it is expected to happen at that time.

check out^{복습}

idiom (책 등을) 빌리다, 대출하다
If you check something out, you borrow it such as a book or a video from a library.

borrow^{복습}
[bárou]

v. (물건 · 돈 · 생각 등을) 빌리다
If you borrow something that belongs to someone else, you take it or use it for a period of time, usually with their permission.

scribble^{복습}
[skribl]

v. 낙서하다; 갈겨쓰다, 휘갈기다; n. 낙서
To scribble means to make meaningless marks or rough drawings using a pencil or pen.

stack^{복습}
[stæk]

n. 더미; 많음, 다량; v. 쌓다, 쌓아올리다
A stack of things is a pile of them.

steal^{복습}
[sti:l]

v. 훔치다, 도둑질하다
If you steal something from someone, you take it away from them without their permission and without intending to return it.

glance ^{복습}
[glæns]

v. 흘긋 보다, 잠깐 보다; n. 흘긋 봄
If you glance at something or someone, you look at them very quickly and then look away again immediately.

jail ^{복습}
[dʒeil]

n. 교도소, 감옥
A jail is a place where criminals are kept in order to punish them, or where people waiting to be tried are kept.

arrest^{**}
[ərést]

v. 체포하다, 저지하다; n. 체포, 검거
If the police arrest you, they take charge of you and take you to a police station, because they believe you may have committed a crime.

master^{**}
[mǽstər]

n. 주인, 대가; v. 지배하다, 숙달하다, 정통하다
A dog's master is the man or boy who owns it.

whip[*]
[hwip]

v. 채찍질하다; 세차게 때리다; 휙 잡아채다; n. 채찍(질), 마부
If someone whips a person or animal, they beat them or hit them with a whip or something like a whip.

trick ^{복습}
[trik]

n. 묘기, 재주; 속임수; 비결, 요령; v. 속이다, 속임수를 쓰다
A trick is a clever or skillful action that someone does in order to entertain people.

smoke^{**}
[smouk]

v. (담배 등을) 피우다, 연기를 내뿜다; n. 연기, 매연
When someone smokes a cigarette or cigar, they suck the smoke from it into their mouth and blow it out again.

swing ^{복습}
[swiŋ]

v. (한 점을 축으로 하여) 빙 돌다, 휙 움직이다; 휘두르다
If something swings in a particular direction or if you swing it in that direction, it moves in that direction with a smooth, curving movement.

tongue ^{복습}
[tʌŋ]

n. 혀
Your tongue is the soft movable part inside your mouth which you use for tasting, eating, and speaking.

bet[*]
[bet]

v. 틀림없이 ~이다, ~라고 확신하다; 걸다, 내기를 하다; n. 내기, 건 돈
You use expressions such as 'I bet', 'I'll bet', and 'you can bet' to indicate that you are sure something is true.

amaze ^{복습}
[əméiz]

v. 깜짝 놀라게 하다 (amazed a. 깜짝 놀란)
If something amazes you, it surprises you very much.

Check Your Reading Speed

1분에 몇 단어를 읽는지 리딩 속도를 측정해보세요.

$$\frac{721 \text{ words}}{\text{reading time ( ) sec}} \times 60 = (\quad) \text{ WPM}$$

Build Your Vocabulary

nasty 복습
[nǽsti]

a. 심술궂은, 비열한; 더러운, 불쾌한 (nastily ad. 심술궂게)
If you describe a person or their behavior as nasty, you mean that they behave in an unkind and unpleasant way.

disturb**
[distə́:rb]

v. 방해하다, 어지럽히다
If you disturb someone, you interrupt what they are doing and upset them.

mimic
[mímik]

v. (mimicked–mimicked) 흉내 내다, 흉내 내어 조롱하다; 꼭 닮다
If you mimic the actions or voice of a person or animal, you imitate them, usually in a way that is meant to be amusing or entertaining.

bet 복습
[bet]

v. 틀림없이 ～이다, ～라고 확신하다; 걸다, 내기를 하다; n. 내기, 건 돈
You use expressions such as 'I bet', 'I'll bet', and 'you can bet' to indicate that you are sure something is true.

arrest 복습
[ərést]

v. 체포하다, 저지하다; n. 체포, 검거
If the police arrest you, they take charge of you and take you to a police station, because they believe you may have committed a crime.

sicken
[síkən]

v. 메스껍게 하다, 넌더리나게 하다; 병나다 (sickening a. 구역질 나게 하는)
If something sickens you, it makes you feel disgusted.

cheat**
[tʃi:t]

v. 속이다; 규칙을 어기다; n. 사기
(cheat someone out of something idiom ～를 속여 ～을 빼앗다)
If someone cheat you out of something, they prevent you from having it, especially in an unfair or dishonest way.

make sense 복습

idiom 뜻이 통하다, 도리에 맞다
If something makes sense, it has a meaning that you can easily understand.

paragraph*
[pǽrəgræf]

n. 문단, 단락
A paragraph is a section of a piece of writing. A paragraph always begins on a new line and contains at least one sentence.

concern**
[kənsə́:rn]

v. 염려하다; ～에 관계하다; 관심을 갖다; n. 염려; 관심 (concerned a. 우려하는)
If something concerns you, it worries you.

organization**
[ɔ̀rgənizéiʃən]

n. 조직, 단체
An organization is an official group of people, for example a political party, a business, a charity, or a club.

112

sort of ^{복습}	idiom 말하자면, 다소, 얼마간 You use sort of when you want to say that your description of something is not very accurate.
flutter ^{복습} [flʌ́tər]	v. (깃발 등이) 펄럭이다, (새 등이) 날갯짓하다; n. 펄럭임 If something thin or light flutters, or if you flutter it, it moves up and down or from side to side with a lot of quick, light movements.
complain ^{복습} [kəmpléin]	v. 불평하다, 투덜거리다 (complaint n. 불평, 불만) If you complain about a situation, you say that you are not satisfied with it.
exclaim ^{복습} [ikskléim]	v. 외치다, 소리치다 If you exclaim, you say or shout something suddenly because of surprise, fear and pleasure.
snicker ^{복습} [sníkər]	v. 낄낄 웃다, 숨죽여 웃다; n. 낄낄 웃음 If you snicker, you laugh quietly in a disrespectful way, for example at something rude or embarrassing.
blush ^{복습} [blʌʃ]	v. 얼굴을 붉히다, (얼굴이) 빨개지다; n. 얼굴을 붉힘, 홍조 When you blush, your face becomes redder than usual because you are ashamed or embarrassed.
prove ^{**} [pru:v]	v. 입증하다, 증명하다 If something proves to be true or to have a particular quality, it becomes clear after a period of time that it is true or has that quality.
crawl ^{**} [krɔːl]	v. 기어가다, 느릿느릿 가다; n. 기어감; 서행 When you crawl, you move forward on your hands and knees.
quit ^{복습} [kwit]	v. 그치다, 그만두다; (술·담배 등을) 끊다 If you quit an activity or quit doing something, you stop doing it.
tease ^{복습} [ti:z]	v. 놀리다, 장난하다; n. 장난, 놀림 To tease someone means to laugh at them or make jokes about them in order to embarrass, annoy, or upset them.
beat ^{복습} [bi:t]	v. (심장이) 고동치다; 치다, 두드리다; 패배시키다, 이기다; n. [음악] 박자, 고동 When your heart or pulse beats, it continually makes regular rhythmic movements.
roar [*] [rɔːr]	v. 크게 웃다; (큰 짐승 등이) 으르렁거리다, 고함치다; n. 으르렁거리는 소리 If someone roars with laughter, they laugh in a very noisy way.
insist ^{복습} [insíst]	v. 우기다, 주장하다; 강요하다 If you insist that something is the case, you say so very firmly and refuse to say otherwise, even though other people do not believe you.
hysterical ^{복습} [histérikəl]	a. 히스테리 상태의, 발작적인 Someone who is hysterical is in a state of uncontrolled excitement, anger, or panic.
emotion ^{**} [imóuʃən]	n. 감정, 정서; 감동, 감격 Emotion is strong feeling such as joy or love.

lie ^{복습}
[lai]

① v. (lay–lain) 눕다, 누워 있다; 놓여 있다, 위치하다 ② v. 거짓말하다; n. 거짓말
If you are lying somewhere, you are in a horizontal position and are not standing or sitting.

stick ^{복습}
[stik]

① v. (stuck–stuck) 내밀다; 찔러 넣다, 찌르다; 붙이다, 달라붙다
② n. 막대기, 지팡이
If something is sticking into a surface or object, it is partly in it.

fire ***
[faiər]

v. 해고하다; 발사하다; 불을 지르다; n. 불, 화재
If an employer fires you, they dismiss you from your job.

for sure

idiom 확실히, 틀림없이
If you say that something is for sure or that you know it for sure, you mean that it is definitely true.

114

1분에 몇 단어를 읽는지 리딩 속도를 측정해보세요.

$$\frac{1,054 \text{ words}}{\text{reading time (\quad) sec}} \times 60 = (\qquad) \text{ WPM}$$

Build Your Vocabulary

attention^{복습}
[əténʃən]

n. 주의, 관심; 배려
If you give someone or something your attention, you look at it, listen to it, or think about it carefully.

arithmetic^{복습}
[əríθmətik]

n. 산수, 셈
Arithmetic is the part of mathematics that is concerned with the addition, subtraction, multiplication, and division of numbers.

nod^{복습}
[nad]

v. 끄덕이다, 끄덕여 표시하다; n. (동의 · 인사 · 신호 · 명령의) 끄덕임
If you nod, you move your head downward and upward to show agreement, understanding, or approval.

nerve^{**}
[nəːrv]

n. 용기; 신경 (조직); v. 용기를 내어 ～하게 하다
(lose one's nerve **idiom** 겁먹다, 기가 죽다)
If you lose your nerve, you suddenly panic and become too afraid to do something that you were about to do.

charm^{**}
[ʧaːrm]

n. 부적, 마법; 매력; v. 주문을 걸다; 매혹하다
A charm is an act, saying, or object that is believed to have magic powers.

borrow^{복습}
[bárou]

v. (물건 · 돈 · 생각 등을) 빌리다
If you borrow something that belongs to someone else, you take it or use it for a period of time, usually with their permission.

fist^{복습}
[fist]

n. (쥔) 주먹
Your hand is referred to as your fist when you have bent your fingers in toward the palm in order to hit someone, to make an angry gesture, or to hold something.

pleasant^{**}
[plézənt]

a. 즐거운, 유쾌한; (날씨가) 쾌적한
Something that is pleasant is nice, enjoyable, or attractive.

principal^{복습}
[prínsəpəl]

n. 장(長), 교장; a. 주요한, 제1의
The principal of a school or a college, is the person in charge of the school or college.

warn^{복습}
[wɔːrn]

v. 경고하다; ～에게 통지하다
If you warn someone about something such as a possible danger or problem, you tell them about it so that they are aware of it.

auditorium^{복습}
[ɔːditɔ́ːriəm]

n. 강당, 회관; 청중석, 관객석
An auditorium is a large room, hall, or building which is used for events such as meetings and concerts.

accidental[복습]
[æksədéntl]

a. 우연한; 부수적인 (accidentally ad. 우연히)
An accidental event happens by chance or as the result of an accident, and is not deliberately intended.

spill[복습]
[spil]

v. 엎지르다, 흘리다; n. 엎지름, 유출
If a liquid spills or if you spill it, it accidentally flows over the edge of a container.

odd**
[ad]

a. 이상한, 기묘한 (oddly ad. 이상하게)
If you describe someone or something as odd, you think that they are strange or unusual.

wallpaper[복습]
[wɔ:lpéipər]

v. (벽 · 천장 등에) 벽지를 바르다; n. 벽지
If someone wallpapers a room, they cover the walls with wallpaper.

garage*
[gərá:dʒ]

n. 차고, 주차장
A garage is a building in which you keep a car.

lock[복습]
[lak]

v. 잠그다; 고정시키다; 가두어 넣다; n. 자물쇠
When you lock something such as a door, drawer, or case, you fasten it, usually with a key, so that other people cannot open it.

driveway
[dráivwèi]

n. (도로에서 집 · 차고까지의) 진입로
A driveway is a piece of hard ground that leads from the road to the front of a house or other building.

paste*
[peist]

n. 풀; 밀가루 반죽; v. 풀로 붙이다
Paste is a soft, wet, sticky mixture of a substance and a liquid, which can be spread easily. Some types of paste are used to stick things together.

put an end to

idiom ~을 그만두게 하다, 종지부를 찍다
To put an end to something means to cause it to stop.

trial*
[traiəl]

n. 재판, 공판; 시험, 실험
A trial is a formal meeting in a law court, at which a judge and jury listen to evidence and decide whether a person is guilty of a crime.

innocent[복습]
[ínəsənt]

a. 잘못이 없는, 결백한; 순진한
Innocent people are those who are not involved in a crime or conflict, but are injured or killed as a result of it.

surround[복습]
[səráund]

v. 둘러싸다, 에워싸다; n. 둘러싸는 것; 환경, 주위
If a person or thing is surrounded by something, that thing is situated all around them.

gang[복습]
[gæŋ]

n. 패거리, 한 떼, 무리
A gang is a group of people who go around together and often deliberately cause trouble.

concrete[복습]
[kánkri:t]

n. 콘크리트; a. 유형의, 구체적인
Concrete is a substance used for building which is made by mixing together cement, sand, small stones, and water.

bounce[복습]
[bauns]

v. 튀다, 튀게 하다; 급히 움직이다, 뛰어다니다; n. 튐, 바운드
When an object such as a ball bounces or when you bounce it, it moves upward from a surface or away from it immediately after hitting it.

116

glance^{복습}
[glæns]

v. 흘긋 보다, 잠깐 보다; n. 흘긋 봄
If you glance at something or someone, you look at them very quickly and then look away again immediately.

block***
[blak]

v. (지나가지 못하게) 막다, 차단하다; n. 사각형 덩어리; (도로로 나뉘는) 구역, 블록
If you block someone's way, you prevent them from going somewhere or entering a place by standing in front of them.

stare^{복습}
[stɛər]

v. 응시하다, 뚫어지게 보다
If you stare at someone or something, you look at them for a long time.

defiant
[difáiənt]

a. 도전적인, 반항적인 (defiantly ad. 도전적으로)
If you say that someone is defiant, you mean they show aggression or independence by refusing to obey someone.

clutch^{복습}
[klʌʧ]

v. 꽉 잡다, 붙들다, 부여잡다; n. 움켜쥠
If you clutch at something or clutch something, you hold it tightly, usually because you are afraid or anxious.

harm**
[haːrm]

v. 해치다, 손상을 입히다; n. 해, 손해
To harm a thing, or sometimes a person, means to damage them or make them less effective or successful than they were.

pal*
[pæl]

n. 친구; 동료; v. 친구가 되다
Your pals are your friends.

chuckle^{복습}
[ʧʌkl]

v. 빙그레 웃다, 소리 없이 웃다
When you chuckle, you laugh quietly.

rest***
[rɛst]

v. 놓다, 얹다; 쉬다, 휴식시키다; n. 휴식
If you rest something somewhere, you put it there so that its weight is supported.

jerk^{복습}
[dʒəːrk]

v. 갑자기 움직이다; n. 갑자기 잡아당김; 바보, 얼간이
If you jerk something or someone in a particular direction, or they jerk in a particular direction, they move a short distance very suddenly and quickly.

back away^{복습}

idiom (~에서) 뒷걸음질치다, (~을) 피하다
If you back away, you move backward away from someone or something frightening or unpleasant.

hold on^{복습}

idiom 기다려
You say 'hold on' to ask someone to wait or stop for a short time.

sincere**
[sinsíəːr]

a. 진실한, 진심의; 성실한, 참된 (sincerely ad. 진심으로)
If you say that someone is sincere, you approve of them because they really mean the things they say.

patch*
[pæʧ]

n. (다른 것과 달라 보이는) 부분; 헝겊 조각; v. 헝겊을 대고 깁다
A patch on a surface is a part of it which is different in appearance from the area around it.

bruise*
[bruːz]

n. 타박상, 멍; v. 멍들게 하다, 타박상을 입히다
A bruise is an injury which appears as a purple mark on your body, although the skin is not broken.

tint
[tint]

n. 엷은 빛깔, 색깔; v. ~에 (연하게) 색칠하다
A tint is a small amount of color.

urge^{복습}
[ə:rdʒ]

v. 촉구하다, 충고하다, 재촉하다; n. (강한) 충동
If you urge someone to do something, you try hard to persuade them to do it.

lower^{**}
[louər]

v. 낮추다, 내리다
If you lower something, you move it slowly downward.

snicker^{복습}
[sníkər]

v. 킬킬 웃다, 숨죽여 웃다; n. 킬킬 웃음
If you snicker, you laugh quietly in a disrespectful way, for example at something rude or embarrassing.

dumbfound
[dʌmfáund]

v. 말문이 막히도록 깜짝 놀라게 하다 (dumbfounded a. 놀라서 말이 안 나오는)
If someone or something dumbfounds you, they surprise you very much.

break the ice

idiom 서먹한 침묵을 깨다, 딱딱한 분위기를 누그러뜨리다
If you break the ice at a party or meeting, or in a new situation, you say or do something to make people feel relaxed and comfortable.

bewilder
[biwíldər]

v. 당황하게 하다, 어리둥절하게 하다 (bewildered a. 당혹한)
If something bewilders you, it is so confusing or difficult that you cannot understand it.

pat[*]
[pæt]

v. 톡톡 가볍게 치다, 쓰다듬다; n. 쓰다듬기
If you pat something or someone, you tap them lightly, usually with your hand held flat.

even^{***}
[í:vən]

a. 대등한; 균등한, 동일한; ad. 한층, 더욱
An even contest or competition is equally balanced between the two sides who are taking part.

chapters 33 to 36

1. Why did Bradley try to take a shot at the basket at the end
   of the game?
   A. His team could have won if he took the shot.
   B. He wanted to show off and make new friends.
   C. Someone on the other team had blocked his pass to Jeff.
   D. The members on both teams sat down and let him take a shot.

2. What happened while Jeff washed his face in the boys'
   bathroom?
   A. Bradley walked in.
   B. Colleen walked in.
   C. Carla walked in.
   D. A teacher walked in.

3. Why was Colleen seeing Carla when Jeff visited her office?
   A. Colleen's parents had finally signed the form.
   B. She still needed advice about her party.
   C. She had gone into the boys' bathroom.
   D. She was thinking about moving to a different school.

4. Why did Colleen say that Jeff should be a Zen monk?
   A. Because he shaved his head and wore a robe.
   B. Because he said hello back to people.
   C. Because he was didn't eat meat.
   D. Because he was calm and peaceful.

5. What did Bradley's father help Bradley with before dinner?
   A. He helped him do homework.
   B. He helped him learn to shoot baskets.
   C. He helped him learn to pass the basketball.
   D. He helped him learn to dribble the basketball.

6. Why did Colleen almost not invite Melinda to her party?
   A. Because Lori was her new best friend.
   B. Because Melinda was bigger than her.
   C. Because Melinda had beat up Bradley and Jeff.
   D. Because Melinda wouldn't give her a present.

7. Why had Bradley not been to a birthday party since the third grade?
   A. Because he had sat in a cake.
   B. Because he had beat up a kid.
   C. Because he had eaten the whole cake.
   D. Because he had stolen the presents.

1분에 몇 단어를 읽는지 리딩 속도를 측정해보세요.

$$\frac{413 \text{ words}}{\text{reading time ( ) sec}} \times 60 = (\qquad) \text{ WPM}$$

Build Your Vocabulary

terrible^{복습}
[térəbl]

a. 형편없는; 심한, 지독한
If something is terrible, it is very bad or of very poor quality.

dribble
[dríbl]

v. 공을 드리블하다; (물방울 등이) 똑똑 떨어지다
When players dribble the ball in a game such as football or basketball, they keep kicking or tapping it quickly in order to keep it moving.

dare*
[dɛər]

v. 감히 ~하다, 무릅쓰다, 도전하다
If you dare to do something, you do something which requires a lot of courage.

shot^{복습}
[ʃat]

n. 시도, 기회; 겨냥, 발사; 주사
If you have a shot at something, you attempt to do it.

tongue^{복습}
[tʌŋ]

n. 혀
Your tongue is the soft movable part inside your mouth which you use for tasting, eating, and speaking.

slip^{복습}
[slip]

v. 살짝 나오다, 살짝 들어가다; 미끄러지다
If something slips, it slides out of place or out of your hand.

aim***
[eim]

v. 겨냥을 하다, 목표삼다; n. 겨냥, 조준; 목적, 뜻
If you aim a weapon or object at something or someone, you point it toward them before firing or throwing it.

rim*
[rim]

n. (둥근 물건의) 가장자리, 테두리; v. 둘러싸다, 테를 두르다
The rim of a circular object is its outside edge.

bounce^{복습}
[bauns]

v. 튀다, 튀게 하다; 급히 움직이다, 뛰어다니다; n. 튐, 바운드
When an object such as a ball bounces or when you bounce it, it moves upwards from a surface or away from it immediately after hitting it.

pat^{복습}
[pæt]

v. 톡톡 가볍게 치다, 쓰다듬다; n. 쓰다듬기
If you pat something or someone, you tap them lightly, usually with your hand held flat.

lie^{복습}
[lai]

① v. 놓여 있다, 위치하다; 눕다, 누워 있다 ② v. 거짓말하다; n. 거짓말
If an object lies in a particular place, it is in a flat position in that place.

no wonder

idiom 조금도 놀랍지 않다
If you say 'no wonder', you mean that something is not surprising.

122

fountain^{복습}
[fáuntən]

n. 분수; 샘
A fountain is an ornamental feature in a pool or lake which consists of a long narrow stream of water that is forced up into the air.

thirsty*
[θə́:rsti]

a. 목마른; 갈망하는, 열망하는
If you are thirsty, you feel a need to drink something.

court^{복습}
[kɔːrt]

n. (테니스 · 배구 등의) 코트; 뜰, 안마당; 법정, 법원
A court is an area in which you play a game such as tennis, basketball, badminton, or squash.

weird^{복습}
[wiərd]

a. 이상한, 기묘한; 수상한
If you describe something or someone as weird, you mean that they are strange.

splash^{복습}
[splæʃ]

v. (물 · 흙탕 등) 튀기다, 첨벙거리다; n. 튀기기; 첨벙 튀기는 소리
If you splash a liquid somewhere or if it splashes, it hits someone or something and scatters in a lot of small drops.

sweat*
[swet]

v. 땀 흘리다; 습기가 차다; n. 땀 (sweaty a. 땀투성이의)
When you sweat, drops of liquid comes through your skin.

faucet*
[fɔ́:sit]

n. (수도 · 통의) 물 꼭지, 물 주둥이
A faucet is a device that controls the flow of a liquid or gas from a pipe or container.

swing^{복습}
[swiŋ]

v. (한 점을 축으로 하여) 빙 돌다, 휙 움직이다; 휘두르다
If something swings in a particular direction or if you swing it in that direction, it moves in that direction with a smooth, curving movement.

1분에 몇 단어를 읽는지 리딩 속도를 측정해보세요.

$$\frac{703 \text{ words}}{\text{reading time ( ) sec}} \times 60 = (\quad) \text{ WPM}$$

Build Your Vocabulary

weird 복습
[wiərd]
a. 이상한, 기묘한; 수상한
If you describe something or someone as weird, you mean that they are strange.

knock 복습
[nak]
v. (문을) 두드리다, 노크하다; 치다, 부수다; n. 노크; 타격
If you knock on something such as a door or window, you hit it, usually several times, to attract someone's attention.

lower 복습
[louər]
v. 낮추다, 내리다
If you lower something, you move it slowly downward.

mutter 복습
[mʌtər]
v. 중얼거리다, 불평하다; n. 중얼거림, 불평
If you mutter, you speak very quietly so that you cannot easily be heard, often because you are complaining about something.

awkward 복습
[ɔ́ːkwərd]
a. 어색한, 불편한, 곤란한 (awkwardly ad. 어색하게)
Someone who feels awkward behaves in a shy or embarrassed way.

peek 복습
[piːk]
v. 살짝 들여다보다, 엿보다; n. 엿봄
If you peek at something or someone, you have a quick look at them.

emergency **
[imə́ːrdʒənsi]
n. 비상사태, 위급함; a. 비상용의, 긴급한
An emergency is an unexpected and difficult or dangerous situation, especially an accident, which happens suddenly and which requires quick action to deal with it.

explode 복습
[iksplóud]
v. 폭발하다, 격발하다; 폭발시키다
If someone explodes, they express strong feelings suddenly and violently.

blush 복습
[blʌʃ]
v. 얼굴을 붉히다, (얼굴이) 빨개지다; n. 얼굴을 붉힘, 홍조
When you blush, your face becomes redder than usual because you are ashamed or embarrassed.

on purpose 복습
idiom 고의로, 일부러
If you do something on purpose, you do it intentionally.

amaze 복습
[əméiz]
v. 깜짝 놀라게 하다 (amazement n. 놀람, 경탄)
If something amazes you, it surprises you very much.

scary 복습
[skéəri]
a. 무서운, 두려운
Something that is scary is rather frightening.

demand 복습
[diménd]

v. 묻다, 요구하다, 청구하다; n. 요구, 수요
If you demand something such as information or action, you ask for it in a very forceful way.

frown 복습
[fraun]

v. 얼굴을 찡그리다, 눈살을 찌푸리다; n. 찌푸린 얼굴
When someone frowns, their eyebrows become drawn together, because they are annoyed or puzzled.

period 복습
[píːəriəd]

n. (학교의 일과를 나눠 놓은) 시간; 기간, 시기
At a school or college, a period is one of the parts that the day is divided into during which lessons or other activities take place.

religion**
[rilídʒən]

n. 종교
Religion is belief in a god or gods and the activities that are connected with this belief.

roof 복습
[ruːf]

n. 지붕
The roof of a building is the covering on top of it that protects the people and things inside from the weather.

beam 복습
[biːm]

n. [건축] 들보, 기둥; 환한 얼굴; 빛줄기; v. 활짝 웃다; 비추다
A beam is a long thick bar of wood, metal, or concrete, especially one used to support the roof of a building.

carpenter*
[káːrpəntər]

n. 목수, 목공
A carpenter is a person whose job is making and repairing wooden things.

monastery
[mánəstèri]

n. (주로 남자의) 수도원
A monastery is a building or collection of buildings in which monks live.

cardinal*
[káːrdənl]

a. 기본적인, 주요한
A cardinal rule or quality is the one that is considered to be the most important.

monk
[mʌŋk]

n. 수도자, 수도승
A monk is a member of a male religious community that is usually separated from the outside world.

latter**
[lǽtər]

a. 마지막의, 후자의; 최근의
When two people, things, or groups have just been mentioned, you can refer to the second of them as the latter.

exclaim 복습
[ikskléim]

v. 외치다, 소리치다
If you exclaim, you say or shout something suddenly because of surprise, fear and pleasure.

delight 복습
[diláit]

n. 기쁨, 즐거움; v. 즐겁게 하다, 매우 기쁘게 하다
Delight is a feeling of very great pleasure.

1분에 몇 단어를 읽는지 리딩 속도를 측정해보세요.

$$\frac{820 \text{ words}}{\text{reading time (} \quad \text{) sec}} \times 60 = (\quad) \text{ WPM}$$

Build Your Vocabulary

and all

idiom ~까지, ~을 포함하여, 게다가
You use and all when you want to emphasize that what you are talking about includes the thing mentioned, especially when this is surprising or unusual.

dribble^{복습}
[dribl]

v. 공을 드리블하다; (물방울 등이) 똑똑 떨어지다
When players dribble the ball in a game such as football or basketball, they keep kicking or tapping it quickly in order to keep it moving.

hardly^{복습}
[háːrdli]

ad. 거의 ~아니다, 전혀 ~않다
When you say you can hardly do something, you are emphasizing that it is very difficult for you to do it.

recess^{복습}
[riːses]

n. (학교의) 쉬는 시간; 휴회
A recess is a short period of time when you have a rest or a change from what you are doing, especially if you are working or if you are in a boring or unpleasant situation.

neat^{복습}
[niːt]

a. 말끔한, 깔끔한; 멋진, 훌륭한 (neatly ad. 깔끔하게)
A neat place, thing, or person is tidy and smart, and has everything in the correct place.

rush^{**}
[rʌʃ]

v. 서두르다, 돌진하다; n. 돌진, 급습
If you rush somewhere, you go there quickly.

stop cold

idiom 갑자기 멈추다, 갑자기 서다
If you stop cold you stop suddenly or abruptly.

determine[*]
[ditɔ́ːrmin]

v. 결심하다, 결정하다 (determination n. 결심, 결의)
If you determine to do something, you make a firm decision to do it.

monk^{복습}
[mʌŋk]

n. 수도자, 수도승
A monk is a member of a male religious community that is usually separated from the outside world.

stare^{복습}
[stɛər]

v. 응시하다, 뚫어지게 보다
If you stare at someone or something, you look at them for a long time.

nod^{복습}
[nad]

v. 끄덕이다, 끄덕여 표시하다; n. (동의 · 인사 · 신호 · 명령의) 끄덕임
If you nod, you move your head downward and upward to show agreement, understanding, or approval.

scoot
[skuːt]

v. 뛰어나가다, 급히 움직이다
If you scoot somewhere, you go there very quickly.

stick^{복습}
[stik]

① v. (stuck-stuck) 내밀다; 찔러 넣다, 찌르다; 붙이다, 달라붙다
② n. 막대기, 지팡이
If something is sticking out from a surface or object, it extends up or away from it.

tongue^{복습}
[tʌŋ]

n. 혀
Your tongue is the soft movable part inside your mouth which you use for tasting, eating, and speaking.

obvious**
[ábviəs]

a. 명백한, 분명한 (obviously ad. 분명히, 명백하게)
If something is obvious, it is easy to see or understand.

beat^{복습}
[bi:t]

v. (beat-beat) 치다, 두드리다; 패배시키다, 이기다; (심장이) 고동치다;
n. [음악] 박자, 고동
If you beat someone or something, you hit them very hard.

reasonable
[rí:zənəbl]

a. 사리를 아는, 분별 있는, 합당한 (unreasonable a. 불합리한)
If you think that someone is fair and sensible, you can say that they are reasonable.

lawyer**
[lɔ́:jər]

n. 변호사, 법률가
A lawyer is a person who is qualified to advise people about the law and represent them in court.

peanut^{복습}
[pí:nʌt]

n. 땅콩
Peanuts are small nuts that grow under the ground. Peanuts are often eaten as a snack, especially roasted and salted.

shrug^{복습}
[ʃrʌg]

v. (양 손바닥을 내보이면서 어깨를) 으쓱하다; n. 으쓱하기
If you shrug, you raise your shoulders to show that you are not interested in something or that you do not know or care about something.

big deal
[big di:l]

intl. 그게 무슨 대수라고!; n. 대단한 것, 큰 일
You can say 'big deal' to someone to show that you are not impressed by something that they consider important or impressive.

time***
[taim]

v. 시간을 재다, 속도를 재다; n. 시간, 때
If you time an action or activity, you measure how long someone takes to do it or how long it lasts.

stay up

idiom (늦게까지) 깨어 있다, 안 자다
If you stay up, you don't go to bed.

admit^{복습}
[ædmít]

v. 인정하다
If you admit that something bad, unpleasant, or embarrassing is true, you agree, often unwillingly, that it is true.

garage^{복습}
[gərá:dʒ]

n. 차고, 주차장
A garage is a building in which you keep a car.

brag
[bræg]

v. 자랑하다, 자만하다, 허풍떨다
If you brag, you say in a very proud way that you have something or have done something.

figure out^{복습}

idiom 계산하다; ~을 생각해내다, 발견하다
If you figure something out, you calculate the total amount of something.

1분에 몇 단어를 읽는지 리딩 속도를 측정해보세요.

$$\frac{1,020 \text{ words}}{\text{reading time (}\quad\text{) sec}} \times 60 = (\quad\quad) \text{ WPM}$$

Build Your Vocabulary

giggle 복습
[gigl]

v. 낄낄 웃다; n. 낄낄 웃음
If someone giggles, they laugh in a childlike way, because they are amused, nervous, or embarrassed.

schedule *
[skédʒuːl]

n. 예정하다, 시간표를 만들다; n. 일정, 계획, 스케줄
If something is scheduled to happen at a particular time, arrangements are made for it to happen at that time.

appointment 복습
[əpɔ́intmənt]

n. 약속, 예약; 지정, 임명
If you have an appointment with someone, you have arranged to see them at a particular time, usually in connection with their work or for a serious purpose.

hall 복습
[hɔːl]

n. (건물 안의) 복도; (건물 입구 안쪽의) 현관
A hall in a building is a long passage with doors into rooms on both sides of it.

beat someone to it 복습

idiom 기선을 제압하다, 선수를 치다
If you intend to do something but someone beats you to it, they do it before you do.

appreciate 복습
[əpríːʃièit]

v. 고맙게 생각하다; 평가하다, 감상하다
If you appreciate something that someone has done for you or is going to do for you, you are grateful for it.

get a kick out of

idiom ~에서 스릴을 얻다, ~이 재미있다
If you get a kick out of something, it makes you feel very excited or very happy for a short period of time.

sort of 복습

idiom 다소, 얼마간, 말하자면
You use sort of when you want to say that your description of something is not very accurate.

beige
[beiʒ]

n. 베이지색(갈색을 띤 엷은 회색)
Something that is beige is pale brown in color.

rotten 복습
[ratn]

a. 썩은, 부패한; 형편없는, 끔찍한
If food, wood, or another substance is rotten, it has decayed and can no longer be used.

blurt
[bləːrt]

v. 불쑥 말하다; 무심결에 누설하다
If someone blurts something, they say it suddenly, after trying hard to keep quiet or to keep it secret.

128

pour^{**}
[pɔːr]

v. 쏟아져 나오다, 흐르다; 따르다, 쏟다, 흘리다
When a liquid or other substance pours somewhere, for example through a hole, it flows quickly and in large quantities.

dribble^{복습}
[dribl]

v. 공을 드리블하다; (물방울 등이) 똑똑 떨어지다
When players dribble the ball in a game such as football or basketball, they keep kicking or tapping it quickly in order to keep it moving.

fortunate^{**}
[fɔ́ːrtʃənət]

a. 운이 좋은, 행운의, 복 받은 (fortunately ad. 다행스럽게도, 운 좋게도)
If you say that someone is fortunate, you mean that they are lucky.

be got to do with

idiom ~와 관계가 있다
If a thing is got to do with someone or something, it is connected or concerned with them or it.

sob^{복습}
[sab]

v. 흐느껴 울다; n. 흐느낌, 오열
When someone sobs, they cry in a noisy way, breathing in short breaths.

tear^{복습}
[tiə:r]

① n. 눈물 ② v. 부리나케 가다; 찢다, 찢어지다; n. 찢음
Tears are the drops of salty liquid that come out of your eyes when you are crying.

spill^{복습}
[spil]

v. 엎지르다, 흘리다; n. 엎지름, 유출
If a liquid spills or if you spill it, it accidentally flows over the edge of a container.

blubber
[blʌ́bər]

v. 엉엉 울다; n. 엉엉 울기; 울보
If someone blubbers, they cry noisily and in an unattractive way.

hiccup
[híkʌp]

v. 딸꾹질을 하다; n. 딸꾹질
When you hiccup, you make repeated sharp sounds in your throat.

blow one's nose

idiom 코를 풀다
When you blow your nose, you force air out of it through your nostrils in order to clear it.

grade^{복습}
[greid]

n. 학년, 등급; 성적, 평점; v. 점수를 매기다, 등급을 매기다
In the United States, a grade is a group of classes in which all the children are of a similar age.

whine
[hwain]

v. 징징거리다, 우는 소리를 하다; (개가) 낑낑거리다
If you say that someone is whining, you mean that they are complaining in an annoying way about something unimportant.

sniffle^{복습}
[snifl]

v. 코를 훌쩍이다, 코를 훌쩍거리며 말하다; n. 코를 훌쩍거림
If you sniffle, you keep sniffing, usually because you are crying or have a cold.

pin^{**}
[pin]

v. 핀으로 꽂다, 고정하다; ~을 꼼짝 못하게 누르다; n. 핀, 장식
If you pin something on or to something, you attach it with a pin, a drawing pin, or a safety pin.

donkey^{복습}
[dánki]

n. [동물] 당나귀
A donkey is an animal which is like a horse but which is smaller and has longer ears.

overwhelm* [òuvərhwélm]

v. 압도하다, 제압하다; 질리게 하다
If you are overwhelmed by a feeling or event, it affects you very strongly, and you do not know how to deal with it.

scare복습 [skɛər]

v. 위협하다, 겁나게 하다
If something scares you, it frightens or worries you.

ball* [bɔːl]

① n. 무도회; v. 즐겁게 보내다 ② n. 공; v. 동그랗게 만들다
A ball is a large formal social event at which people dance.

pumpkin* [pʌ́mpkin]

n. 호박
A pumpkin is a large, round, orange vegetable with a thick skin.

wipe복습 [waip]

v. 닦다, 닦아 내다; n. 닦기
If you wipe something, you rub its surface to remove dirt or liquid from it.

fairy tale [fɛ́əri tèil]

n. 동화, 옛날이야기
A fairy tale is a story for children involving magical events and imaginary creatures.

celebrate** [séləbrèit]

v. 기념하다, 축하하다
If you celebrate, you do something enjoyable because of a special occasion.

1. Which of the following was NOT one of the complaints made by parents about Carla?
   A. They said that Carla cost too much and they could buy computers if they fired her.
   B. They said that Carla had told a student that it was good to fail.
   C. They said that Carla was teaching students to disobey their parents.
   D. They said that Carla was trying to make students change religions.

2. What kind of situation did the parents ask for Carla's opinion?
   A. They wanted to know what she would do if a student bit a teacher.
   B. They wanted to know what she would do if a student punched a teacher.
   C. They wanted to know what she would do if a student stole from a teacher.
   D. They wanted to know what she would do if a student said bad words to a teacher.

3. What news did Carla have for Bradley?
   A. The school was getting new computers for their classrooms.
   B. She was transferring to teach at a different school.
   C. She could help him practice basketball.
   D. He was moving to another classroom.

4. How did Bradley react to Carla's news?

    A. He cried and hugged Carla.

    B. He said that he would miss her.

    C. He pretended not to care about it.

    D. He yelled and told Carla he hated her.

5. Why did Bradley's animals take a vote?

    A. They decided they didn't like Ronnie anymore.

    B. They decided to make Ronnie their leader.

    C. They decided to push Ronnie off the cliff.

    D. They decided to break Ronnie's other ear.

6. Why did Bradley receive a gold star?

    A. He had gotten 100% on the arithmetic test.

    B. He had gone a week without beating up another kid.

    C. Carla had taped his book report together and turned it in.

    D. Carla had written a note to Mrs. Ebbel asking for a gold star.

7. What did Bradley do after school when Carla waited for him?

    A. He went to her office but Carla was already gone.

    B. He walked directly home when the final bell rang.

    C. He went to go play basketball with his friends.

    D. He went home to talk to his animals.

Check Your Reading Speed

1분에 몇 단어를 읽는지 리딩 속도를 측정해보세요.

$$\frac{1{,}123 \text{ words}}{\text{reading time ( ) sec}} \times 60 = (\qquad) \text{ WPM}$$

Build Your Vocabulary

concern 복습
[kənsə́:rn]

v. 염려하다; ~에 관계하다; 관심을 갖다; n. 염려; 관심 (concerned a. 우려하는)
If something concerns you, it worries you.

organization 복습
[ɔ̀rgənizéiʃən]

n. 조직, 단체
An organization is an official group of people, for example a political party, a business, a charity, or a club.

ankle*
[ǽŋkl]

n. 발목
Your ankle is the joint where your foot joins your leg.

fold 복습
[fould]

v. (손·팔·다리를) 끼다, 포개다; 접다, 접어 포개다
If you fold your arms or hands, you bring them together and cross or link them, for example over your chest.

lap**
[læp]

① n. 무릎 ② n. 한 바퀴; v. 겹치게 하다
If you have something on your lap, it is on top of your legs and near to your body.

principal 복습
[prínsəpəl]

n. 장(長), 교장; a. 주요한, 제1의
The principal of a school or a college, is the person in charge of the school or college.

complain 복습
[kəmpléin]

v. 불평하다, 투덜거리다 (complaint n. 불평, 불만)
If you complain about a situation, you say that you are not satisfied with it.

counsel 복습
[káunsəl]

v. 상담을 하다; n. 조언, 충고 (counselor n. 지도교사, 상담사)
If you counsel people, you give them advice about their problems.

discipline**
[dísəplin]

n. 규율, 훈련; v. 훈련하다
Discipline is the practice of making people obey rules or standards of behavior, and punishing them when they do not.

punish***
[pʌ́niʃ]

v. 벌하다, 응징하다, 처벌하다
To punish someone means to make them suffer in some way because they have done something wrong.

clap 복습
[klæp]

v. 박수를 치다; n. 박수
When you clap, you hit your hands together to show appreciation or attract attention.

134

get back to basics

idiom 기본으로 돌아가다
If you talk about getting back to basics, you are suggesting that people have become too concerned with complicated details or new theories, and that they should concentrate on simple, important ideas or activities.

arithmetic^{복습}
[əríθmətik]

n. 산수, 셈
Arithmetic is the part of mathematics that is concerned with the addition, subtraction, multiplication, and division of numbers.

fire^{복습}
[faiər]

v. 해고하다; 발사하다; 불을 지르다; n. 불, 화재
If an employer fires you, they dismiss you from your job.

purpose^{**}
[pə́:rpəs]

n. 목적, 의도; v. 의도하다, 꾀하다
The purpose of something is the reason for which it is made or done.

fail^{복습}
[feil]

v. 실패하다, ~하지 못하다
If you fail to do something that you were trying to do, you are unable to do it or do not succeed in doing it.

relax^{**}
[rilǽks]

v. 편하게 하다, 쉬게 하다; (긴장 등을) 늦추다, 느슨해지다
If you relax or if something relaxes you, you feel more calm and less worried or tense.

pressure^{**}
[préʃər]

n. 압박, 압력; v. 압력을 가하다, 강요하다
If you are under pressure, you are made to feel anxious about something you have to do.

remind^{복습}
[rimáind]

v. 생각나게 하다, 상기시키다, 일깨우다
If someone reminds you of a fact or event that you already know about, they say something which makes you think about it.

permit^{복습}
[pərmít]

v. 허가하다, 허락하다 (permission n. 허락, 허가)
If someone permit you to do something, they allow you to do it.

tax^{**}
[tæks]

n. 세금, 부담; v. 과세하다
Tax is an amount of money that you have to pay to the government so that it can pay for public services.

admit^{복습}
[ædmít]

v. 인정하다
If you admit that something bad, unpleasant, or embarrassing is true, you agree, often unwillingly, that it is true.

emergency^{복습}
[imə́:rdʒənsi]

n. 비상사태, 위급함; a. 비상용의, 긴급한
An emergency is an unexpected and difficult or dangerous situation, especially an accident, which happens suddenly and which requires quick action to deal with it.

personal^{**}
[pə́rsənl]

a. 개인의, 사사로운
Personal matters relate to your feelings, relationships, and health.

justify[*]
[dʒʌ́stəfài]

v. 정당화하다, 변명하다 (justified a. 정당한 이유가 있는, 정당한)
If you think that someone is justified in doing something, you think that their reasons for doing it are good and valid.

religion^{복습}
[rilídʒən]

n. 종교
Religion is belief in a god or gods and the activities that are connected with this belief.

announce^{복습}
[ənáuns]

v. 발표하다, 알리다
If you announce a piece of news or an intention, especially something that people may not like, you say it loudly and clearly, so that everyone you are with can hear it.

monk^{복습}
[mʌŋk]

n. 수도자, 수도승
A monk is a member of a male religious community that is usually separated from the outside world.

have (got) to do with^{복습}

idiom ~와 관계가 있다
If a thing has to do with someone or something, it is connected or concerned with them or it.

allow^{복습}
[əláu]

v. 허락하다, ~하게 두다; 인정하다
If someone is allowed to do something, it is all right for them to do it and they will not get into trouble.

in the first place

idiom 우선, 맨 먼저
You say in the first place when you are talking about the beginning of a situation or about the situation as it was before a series of events.

apologize**
[əpálədʒàiz]

v. 사과하다, 사죄하다
When you apologize to someone, you say that you are sorry that you have hurt them or caused trouble for them.

assure^{복습}
[əʃúər]

v. 단언하다, 확신하다, 보증하다
If you assure someone that something is true or will happen, you tell them that it is definitely true or will definitely happen, often in order to make them less worried.

row^{복습}
[rou]

① n. 열, 줄 ② v. 노를 젓다, 배를 젓다; n. 노 젓기
A row of things or people is a number of them arranged in a line.

exact^{복습}
[igzǽkt]

a. 정확한, 정밀한 (exactly ad. 정확하게, 꼭)
Exact means correct in every detail.

figure out^{복습}

idiom ~을 생각해내다, 발견하다; 계산하다
If you figure out a solution to a problem or the reason for something, you succeed in solving it or understanding it.

bite^{복습}
[bait]

v. (bit-bit) 물다, 물어뜯다; n. 물기; 한 입(의 분량)
If an animal or person bites you, they use their teeth to hurt or injure you.

exclaim^{복습}
[ikskléim]

v. 외치다, 소리치다
If you exclaim, you say or shout something suddenly because of surprise, fear and pleasure.

sneak^{복습}
[sni:k]

v. 살금살금 가다, 몰래 가다
If you sneak somewhere, you go there very quietly on foot, trying to avoid being seen or heard.

butt
[bʌt]

n. (구어) 엉덩이; 뭉툭한 끝 부분
Someone's butt is their bottom.

ridiculous**
[ridíkjuləs]

a. 터무니없는; 웃기는, 우스꽝스러운
If you say that something or someone is ridiculous, you mean that they are very foolish.

136

sigh^{복습}
[sai]

v. 한숨 쉬다; n. 한숨, 탄식
When you sigh, you let out a deep breath, as a way of expressing feelings such as disappointment, tiredness, or pleasure.

conclude**
[kənklú:d]

v. 결론짓다, 끝내다; 말을 맺다 (conclusion n. 결론, 결과)
If you conclude that something is true, you decide that it is true using the facts you know as a basis.

meanwhile*
[mí:nwàil]

ad. (다른 일이 일어나고 있는) 그 동안에
Meanwhile means while a particular thing is happening.

shot^{복습}
[ʃat]

n. 주사; 시도, 기회; 겨냥, 발사
A shot of a drug is an injection of it.

bet^{복습}
[bet]

v. 틀림없이 ~이다, ~라고 확신하다; 걸다, 내기를 하다; n. 내기, 건 돈
You use expressions such as 'I bet', 'I'll bet', and 'you can bet' to indicate that you are sure something is true.

horrible^{복습}
[hɔ́:rəbl]

a. 끔찍한, 소름 끼치게 싫은; 무서운
You can call something horrible when it causes you to feel great shock, fear, and disgust.

1분에 몇 단어를 읽는지 리딩 속도를 측정해보세요.

$$\frac{1{,}321 \text{ words}}{\text{reading time ( ) sec}} \times 60 = (\qquad) \text{ WPM}$$

Build Your Vocabulary

author**
[ɔ́:θər]

n. 저자, 작자; v. 저술하다, 쓰다
The author of a piece of writing is the person who wrote it.

jail^{복습}
[dʒeil]

n. 교도소, 감옥
A jail is a place where criminals are kept in order to punish them, or where people waiting to be tried are kept.

innocent^{복습}
[ínəsənt]

a. 잘못이 없는, 결백한; 순진한
Innocent people are those who are not involved in a crime or conflict, but are injured or killed as a result of it.

wallpaper^{복습}
[wɔ́:lpéipər]

n. 벽지; v. (벽 · 천장 등에) 벽지를 바르다
Wallpaper is thick colored or patterned paper that is used for covering and decorating the walls of rooms.

garage^{복습}
[gərá:dʒ]

n. 차고, 주차장
A garage is a building in which you keep a car.

lawyer^{복습}
[lɔ́:jər]

n. 변호사, 법률가
A lawyer is a person who is qualified to advise people about the law and represent them in court.

court^{복습}
[kɔ:rt]

n. 법정, 법원; (테니스 · 배구 등의) 코트; 뜰, 안마당
A court is a place where legal matters are decided by a judge and jury.

peanut^{복습}
[pí:nʌt]

n. 땅콩
Peanuts are small nuts that grow under the ground. Peanuts are often eaten as a snack, especially roasted and salted.

absolutely*
[æbsəlú:tli]

ad. 전적으로, 틀림없이
Absolutely means totally and completely.

capture*
[kǽptʃər]

v. 포착하다; 붙잡다, 사로잡다; n. 포획; 포착
If you capture someone or something, you catch them, especially in a war.

essence*
[esns]

n. 본질, 정수, 핵심
The essence of something is its basic and most important characteristic which gives it its individual identity.

rip^{복습}
[rip]

v. 찢다, 벗겨내다; n. 찢어진 틈, 잡아 찢음
When something rips or when you rip it, you tear it forcefully with your hands or with a tool such as a knife.

fluffy
[flʌ́fi]

a. 푹신한, 보풀의, 솜털의
If you describe something such as a towel or a toy animal as fluffy, you mean that it is very soft.

fingerprint
[fíŋgərprìnt]

n. 지문
Fingerprints are marks made by a person's fingers which show the lines on the skin. Everyone's fingerprints are different, so they can be used to identify criminals.

trunk^{복습}
[trʌŋk]

n. 코끼리 코; 여행 가방; (나무의) 줄기, 몸뚱이
An elephant's trunk is its very long nose that it uses to lift food and water to its mouth.

spill^{복습}
[spil]

v. 엎지르다, 흘리다; n. 엎지름, 유출
If a liquid spills or if you spill it, it accidentally flows over the edge of a container.

wipe^{복습}
[waip]

v. 닦다, 닦아 내다; n. 닦기
If you wipe something, you rub its surface to remove dirt or liquid from it.

tremble^{복습}
[trembl]

v. 떨다, 떨리다
If you tremble, you shake slightly because you are frightened or cold.

nod^{복습}
[nad]

v. 끄덕이다, 끄덕여 표시하다; n. (동의 · 인사 · 신호 · 명령의) 끄덕임
If you nod, you move your head downward and upward to show agreement, understanding, or approval.

transfer[*]
[trænsfɔ́:r]

v. 옮기다, 이동하다; 갈아타다; n. 이동; 환승
If you transfer something or someone from one place to another, they go from the first place to the second.

kindergarten
[kíndərgà:rtn]

n. 유치원
A kindergarten is an informal kind of school for very young children, where they learn things by playing.

glisten^{복습}
[glisn]

v. 반짝이다, 반짝반짝 빛나다; n. 반짝임
If something glistens, it shines, usually because it is wet or oily.

on one's own

idiom 혼자, 혼자 힘으로
If you do something on your own, you do it without any help from other people.

trick^{복습}
[trik]

v. 속이다, 속임수를 쓰다; n. 속임수; 비결, 요령; 묘기, 재주
If someone tricks you, they deceive you, often in order to make you do something.

stretch^{복습}
[streʧ]

v. 늘이다; 늘어지다; 기지개를 켜다; (팔 · 다리의 근육을) 당기다; n. 기지개 켜기
When something soft or elastic stretches or is stretched, it becomes longer or bigger as well as thinner, usually because it is pulled.

frown^{복습}
[fraun]

n. 찌푸린 얼굴; v. 얼굴을 찡그리다, 눈살을 찌푸리다
A frown is a look that your face makes with your eyebrows drawn together because you are annoyed or puzzled.

lean^{복습}
[li:n]

v. 기울다, 기울이다, (몸을) 숙이다; ~에 기대다; ~을 ~에 기대 놓다
When you lean in a particular direction, you bend your body in that direction.

sink^{복습}
[siŋk]

n. 세면대; (부엌의) 싱크대, 개수대; v. 가라앉다, 빠지다
A sink is a large bowl, usually with taps for hot and cold water, for washing your hands and face.

throb[*]
[θrɑb]

v. 욱신거리다; (심장이) 고동치다, 맥이 뛰다; n. 고동, 맥박
If part of your body throbs, you feel a series of strong and usually painful beats there.

drain[*]
[drein]

n. 배수관; v. 물을 빼내다, (액체가) 흘러나가다
A drain is a pipe that carries water or sewage away from a place, or an opening in a surface that leads to the pipe.

knock^{복습}
[nɑk]

n. 노크; 타격; v. (문을) 두드리다, 노크하다; 치다, 부수다
A knock is the sound of hitting a door or window, usually several times.

yell^{복습}
[jel]

v. 소리치다, 고함치다; n. 고함소리, 부르짖음
If you yell, you shout loudly, usually because you are excited, angry, or in pain.

handle^{**}
[hændl]

v. 다루다, 처리하다; 대다; n. 손잡이, 핸들
If you say that someone can handle a problem or situation, you mean that they have the ability to deal with it successfully.

fail^{복습}
[feil]

v. 실패하다, ~하지 못하다
If you fail to do something that you were trying to do, you are unable to do it or do not succeed in doing it.

afterward[*]
[æftərwərd]

ad. 후에, 나중에
If you do something or if something happens afterward, you do it or it happens after a particular event or time that has already been mentioned.

toilet^{복습}
[tɔ́ilit]

n. 변기; 화장실
A toilet is a large bowl with a seat, or a platform with a hole, which is connected to a water system and which you use when you want to get rid of urine or feces from your body.

1분에 몇 단어를 읽는지 리딩 속도를 측정해보세요.

$$\frac{101 \text{ words}}{\text{reading time ( ) sec}} \times 60 = (\quad) \text{ WPM}$$

Build Your Vocabulary

hop^{복습}
[hap]

v. 깡충 뛰다, 뛰어오르다; n. 깡충깡충 뜀
If you hop, you move along by jumping.

gather**
[gǽðər]

v. 모이다, 집합하다; 모으다, 끌다
If people gather somewhere or if someone gathers people somewhere, they come together in a group.

vote^{복습}
[vout]

n. 투표, 투표권; v. 투표하다
A vote is a choice made by a particular person or group in a meeting or an election.

sink^{복습}
[siŋk]

v. (sank–sunk) 가라앉다, 빠지다; n. (부엌의) 싱크대, 개수대; 세면대
If something sinks, it moves slowly downward.

Check Your Reading Speed

1분에 몇 단어를 읽는지 리딩 속도를 측정해보세요.

$$\frac{654 \text{ words}}{\text{reading time ( ) sec}} \times 60 = (\qquad) \text{ WPM}$$

Build Your Vocabulary

temperature**
[témpərəʧər]
n. 체온; 온도, 기온
Your temperature is the temperature of your body.

normal^{복습}
[nɔ́ːrməl]
a. 보통의, 정상의, 평범한
Something that is normal is usual and ordinary, and is what people expect.

argue***
[áːrgjuː]
v. 논쟁하다, 주장하다
If one person argues with another, they speak angrily to each other about something that they disagree about.

bizarre
[bizáːr]
a. 기괴한, 별난
Something that is bizarre is very odd and strange.

stomach^{복습}
[stʌ́mək]
n. 배, 복부; 위
You can refer to the front part of your body below your waist as your stomach.

tie^{복습}
[tai]
v. 매다, 끈을 묶다; n. 넥타이
If you tie a piece of string or cloth around something or tie something with a piece of string or cloth, you put the piece of string or cloth around it and fasten the ends together.

knot**
[nat]
n. 매듭; v. 얽히게 하다, 매다
If you tie a knot in a piece of string, rope, cloth, or other material, you pass one end or part of it through a loop and pull it tight.

loosen^{복습}
[luːsn]
v. 풀다, 느슨해지다
If you loosen your grip on something, or if your grip loosens, you hold it less tightly.

drag^{복습}
[dræg]
v. 끌다, 힘들게 움직이다; n. 견인, 끌기
If you drag something, you pull it along the ground.

wave away
idiom 손을 저어 거절하다, 몰아내다
If you wave something away, you do not accept it because you think it is not important or necessary.

accidental^{복습}
[æksədéntl]
a. 우연한; 부수적인 (accidentally ad. 우연히)
An accidental event happens by chance or as the result of an accident, and is not deliberately intended.

stare^{복습}
[stɛər]
v. 응시하다, 뚫어지게 보다
If you stare at someone or something, you look at them for a long time.

amaze^{복습}
[əméiz]

v. 깜짝 놀라게 하다 (amazed a. 깜짝 놀람)
If something amazes you, it surprises you very much.

tape^{복습}
[teip]

v. (접착) 테이프로 붙이다; 녹음하다, 녹화하다; n. (소리 · 영상을 기록하는) 테이프;
(접착용) 테이프
If you tape one thing to another, you attach it using sticky strip of plastic.

lie^{복습}
[lai]

① v. 놓여 있다, 위치하다; 눕다, 누워 있다 ② v. 거짓말하다; n. 거짓말
If an object lies in a particular place, it is in a flat position in that place.

jerk^{복습}
[dʒəːrk]

v. 갑자기 움직이다; n. 갑자기 잡아당김; 바보, 얼간이
If you jerk something or someone in a particular direction, or they jerk in a particular direction, they move a short distance very suddenly and quickly.

remind^{복습}
[rimáind]

v. 생각나게 하다, 상기시키다, 일깨우다
If someone reminds you of a fact or event that you already know about, they say something which makes you think about it.

liar^{복습}
[laiər]

n. 거짓말쟁이
If you say that someone is a liar, you mean that they tell lies.

shove^{복습}
[ʃʌv]

v. (아무렇게나) 밀어넣다; 밀치다, 떠밀다; n. 밀치기
If you shove something somewhere, you push it there quickly and carelessly.

recess^{복습}
[ríːses]

n. (학교의) 쉬는 시간; 휴회
A recess is a short period of time when you have a rest or a change from what you are doing, especially if you are working or if you are in a boring or unpleasant situation.

court^{복습}
[kɔːrt]

n. (테니스 · 배구 등의) 코트; 뜰, 안마당; 법정, 법원
A court is an area in which you play a game such as tennis, basketball, badminton, or squash.

pretend^{복습}
[priténd]

v. ~인 체하다, 가장하다; a. 가짜의, 꾸민
If you pretend that something is the case, you act in a way that is intended to make people believe that it is the case, although in fact it is not.

hall^{복습}
[hɔːl]

n. (건물 안의) 복도; (건물 입구 안쪽의) 현관
A hall in a building is a long passage with doors into rooms on both sides of it.

choke**
[tʃouk]

v. 질식시키다, 숨이 막히다; n. 질식
When you choke or when something chokes you, you cannot breathe properly or get enough air into your lungs.

vocal cords
[vóukəl kɔːrdz]

n. 성대, 목청
Your vocal cords are the part of your throat that vibrates when you speak.

stick^{복습}
[stik]

① v. (stuck-stuck) 찔러 넣다, 찌르다; 붙이다, 달라붙다; 내밀다
② n. 막대기, 지팡이
If you stick something somewhere, you put it there in a rather casual way.

grade^{복습}
[greid]

n. 학년, 등급; 성적, 평점; v. 점수를 매기다, 등급을 매기다

In the United States, a grade is a group of classes in which all the children are of a similar age.

appreciate^{복습}
[əpríːʃièit]

v. 고맙게 생각하다; 평가하다, 감상하다

If you appreciate something that someone has done for you or is going to do for you, you are grateful for it.

tighten[*]
[taitn]

v. 단단해지다, 죄다, 조이다

If you tighten your grip on something, or if your grip tightens, you hold the thing more firmly or securely.

1. Why was Bradley going to a real barber shop instead of having his mother cut his hair?
   A. He complained that his mother made his hair look like a chili bowl.
   B. He wanted to be like Jeff who always had his hair cut at a barber shop.
   C. He had received a discount for a haircut.
   D. He wanted to look nice for Carla.

2. What did Bradley want to do when they arrived at the barber shop?
   A. He wanted to go to the library to check out a book.
   B. He wanted to go to a restaurant to see Carla.
   C. He wanted to go to school to see Carla.
   D. He wanted to go to a different barber shop.

3. What was in the envelope in Carla's office?
   A. Bradley's book report
   B. A book and a letter
   C. Mismatched socks
   D. A card for Bradley

4. What did Bradley's father suggest Bradley do?
   A. He suggested finding another counselor.
   B. He suggested playing basketball together.
   C. He suggested visiting Carla at her new school.
   D. He suggested writing a letter to Carla.

5. Why did the party get quiet after Colleen mentioned a three-legged race?
   A. Each girl wondered if they would run it with a friend.
   B. Each girl wondered if they would get their clothes dirty.
   C. Each girl wondered if they would run it with a boy.
   D. Each girl wondered if they would win.

6. Why did Bradley cut a hole in his pants?
   A. He did it accidentally.
   B. His mother told him to change his pants.
   C. Jeff told him to cut a hole in his pants for the party.
   D. He thought that he needed torn pants for the party.

7. What did Jeff teach Bradley on the way to the party?
   A. Jeff taught Bradley what to do at a birthday party.
   B. Jeff taught Bradley how to play basketball well.
   C. Jeff taught Bradley what to study for their next test.
   D. Jeff taught Bradley how to politely talk to girls.

1분에 몇 단어를 읽는지 리딩 속도를 측정해보세요.

$$\frac{1{,}456 \text{ words}}{\text{reading time (}\qquad\text{) sec}} \times 60 = (\qquad) \text{ WPM}$$

Build Your Vocabulary

be off
idiom 떠나다, 출발하다
If you are off to somewhere, you go there, especially in a hurry.

barber 복습
[báːrbər]
n. 이발사
A barber is a man whose job is cutting men's hair.

complain 복습
[kəmpléin]
v. 불평하다, 투덜거리다
If you complain about a situation, you say that you are not satisfied with it.

snap 복습
[snæp]
v. (화난 목소리로) 딱딱거리다; 딱[툭] (하고) 부러뜨리다, 부러지다
If someone snaps at you, they speak to you in a sharp, unfriendly way.

appreciate 복습
[əpríːʃièit]
v. 고맙게 생각하다; 평가하다, 감상하다
If you appreciate something that someone has done for you or is going to do for you, you are grateful for it.

knot 복습
[nat]
n. 매듭; v. 얽히게 하다, 매다
If you tie a knot in a piece of string, rope, cloth, or other material, you pass one end or part of it through a loop and pull it tight.

stomach 복습
[stʌmək]
n. 배, 복부; 위
You can refer to the front part of your body below your waist as your stomach.

tighten 복습
[taitn]
v. 단단해지다, 죄다, 조이다
If you tighten your grip on something, or if your grip tightens, you hold the thing more firmly or securely.

knock 복습
[nak]
v. (문을) 두드리다, 노크하다; 치다, 부수다; n. 노크; 타격
If you knock on something such as a door or window, you hit it, usually several times, to attract someone's attention.

bother 복습
[báðər]
v. 귀찮게 하다, 괴롭히다; 일부러 ～하다, 애를 쓰다
If someone bothers you, they talk to you when you want to be left alone or interrupt you when you are busy.

counsel 복습
[káunsəl]
v. 상담을 하다; n. 조언, 충고 (counselor n. 지도교사, 상담사)
If you counsel people, you give them advice about their problems.

transfer 복습
[trænsfɔ́ːr]
v. 옮기다, 이동하다; 갈아타다; n. 이동; 환승
If you transfer something or someone from one place to another, they go from the first place to the second.

148

swerve
[swəːrv]

v. 휙 방향을 틀다, 벗어나다, 빗나가다; n. 벗어남, 빗나감
If a vehicle or other moving thing swerves or if you swerve it, it suddenly changes direction, often in order to avoid hitting something.

exclaim^{복습}
[ikskléim]

v. 외치다, 소리치다
If you exclaim, you say or shout something suddenly because of surprise, fear and pleasure.

sick and tired of

idiom ~에 진절머리가 나다
If you are sick and tired of something, it has been going on for a long time and you can no longer tolerate it.

nonsense^{복습}
[nánsens]

n. 허튼소리; 바보 같은 짓; a. 어리석은, 무의미한
If you say that something spoken or written is nonsense, you mean that you consider it to be untrue or silly.

stern[*]
[stəːrn]

a. 엄한, 단호한 (sternly ad. 엄격하게)
Someone who is stern is very serious and strict.

reluctant^{복습}
[rilʌ́ktənt]

a. 꺼리는, 마지못해 하는, 주저하는 (reluctantly ad. 마지못해서, 꺼려하여)
If you are reluctant to do something, you are unwilling to do it and hesitate before doing it, or do it slowly and without enthusiasm.

oily
[ɔ́ili]

a. 기름의, 기름기가 많은
Oily means looking, feeling, tasting, or smelling like oil.

stale[*]
[steil]

a. 퀴퀴한, (좋지 못한) 냄새가 나는; 신선하지 않은
Stale air or a stale smells is unpleasant because it is no longer fresh.

reflect^{**}
[riflékt]

v. 비추다; 반사하다, 반영하다
When something is reflected in a mirror or in water, you can see its image in the mirror or in the water.

multiply^{복습}
[mʌ́ltiplai]

v. 곱하다, 늘리다, 증가하다
When something multiplies or when you multiply it, it increases greatly in number or amount.

back and forth

idiom 앞뒤로, 좌우로
Back and forth means in one direction and then in the opposite one, repeatedly.

awful^{**}
[ɔ́ːfəl]

a. 몹시 나쁜, 지독한; 무서운; ad. 몹시
If you say that something is awful, you mean that it is extremely unpleasant, shocking, or bad.

horrible^{복습}
[hɔ́ːrəbl]

a. 끔찍한, 소름 끼치게 싫은; 무서운
You can call something horrible when it causes you to feel great shock, fear, and disgust.

dungeon
[dʌ́ndʒən]

n. 지하 감옥; v. 지하 감옥에 가두다
A dungeon is a dark underground prison in a castle.

torture[*]
[tɔ́ːrtʃər]

v. 고문하다, 고통을 주다; n. 고문, 고뇌
To torture someone means to cause them to suffer mental pain or anxiety.

occupy*
[ákjupài]

v. 차지하다, 점령하다; 종사하다
If a room or something such as a seat is occupied, someone is using it, so that it is not available for anyone else.

tear복습
[tɛər]

① v. (tore-torn) 찢다, 찢어지다; n. 찢음 ② n. 눈물
If you tear paper, cloth, or another material, or if it tears, you pull it into two pieces or you pull it so that a hole appears in it.

couch*
[kauʧ]

n. 긴 의자, 소파
A couch is a long, comfortable seat for two or three people.

comic*
[kámik]

n. 만화책, 만화잡지; a. 웃기는, 재미있는
A comic book is a magazine that contains stories told in pictures.

slippery복습
[slípəri]

a. 미끄러운, 미끈거리는
Something that is slippery is smooth, wet, or oily and is therefore difficult to walk on or to hold.

apron*
[éiprən]

n. 앞치마
An apron is a piece of clothing that you put on over the front of your normal clothes and tie round your waist, especially when you are cooking.

choke복습
[ʧouk]

v. 질식시키다, 숨이 막히다; n. 질식
When you choke or when something chokes you, you cannot breathe properly or get enough air into your lungs.

comb복습
[koum]

v. (머리카락 · 동물의 털 따위를) 빗질하다, 빗다; n. 빗
When you comb your hair, you tidy it using a comb.

scissors복습
[sízərz]

n. 가위
Scissors are a small cutting tool with two sharp blades that are screwed together.

snip
[snip]

v. (가위로) 자르다, 싹둑 베다; n. 싹둑 자름, 가위질
If you snip something, you cut it quickly using sharp scissors.

filmy
[fílmi]

a. 얇은 막으로 덮인, 희미한
A filmy fabric or substance is very thin and almost transparent.

grit복습
[grit]

v. 이를 갈다; 쓸리다, 삐걱삐걱 (소리 나게) 하다
If you grit your teeth, you press your upper and lower teeth tightly together, usually because you are angry about something.

junk복습
[dʒʌŋk]

n. 쓸모 없는 물건, 쓰레기
Junk is old and used goods that have little value and that you do not want any more.

unhook
[ʌnhúk]

v. 걸쇠를 끄르다, 벗기다
If you unhook a piece of clothing that is fastened with hooks, you undo the hooks.

be through

idiom (일을) 끝마치다
If you are through, you have finished doing something.

still***
[stil]

a. 정지한, 움직이지 않는; 조용한, 고요한; ad. 여전히, 아직도
If you stay still, you stay in the same position and do not move.

150

vacuum[*] [vǽkjuəm]	n. 진공; v. 진공청소기로 청소하다 (vacuum cleaner n. 진공청소기) A vacuum cleaner or a vacuum is an electric machine which sucks up dust and dirt from carpets.
offer^{복습} [ɔ́:fər]	v. 제공하다; 제의하다, 제안하다; n. 제공 If you offer someone something, you give it to them, usually because you feel that they need it or deserve it.
nod^{복습} [nad]	v. 끄덕이다, 끄덕여 표시하다; n. (동의 · 인사 · 신호 · 명령의) 끄덕임 If you nod, you move your head downward and upward to show agreement, understanding, or approval.
lock^{복습} [lak]	v. 잠그다; 고정시키다; 가두어 넣다; n. 자물쇠 When you lock something such as a door, drawer, or case, you fasten it, usually with a key, so that other people cannot open it.
janitor [dʒǽnitər]	n. 수위, 관리인 A janitor is a person whose job is to look after a building.
wax[*] [wæks]	v. 왁스로 닦다, 왁스를 바르다; n. 왁스 If you wax a surface, you put a thin layer of wax onto it, especially in order to polish it.
pound^{복습} [paund]	① v. 마구 치다, 세게 두드리다, 쿵쿵 울리다; n. 타격 ② n. 파운드(무게의 단위) ③ n. 울타리, 우리 If you pound something or pound on it, you hit it with great force, usually loudly and repeatedly.
scowl [skaul]	v. 얼굴을 찌푸리다, 싫은 기색을 하다; n. 찌푸린 얼굴 When someone scowls, an angry or hostile expression appears on their face.
duck^{복습} [dʌk]	① v. 피하다, 머리를 홱 숙이다 ② n. 오리 If you duck, you move your head or the top half of your body quickly downward to avoid something that might hit you, or to avoid being seen.
envelope[*] [énvəlòup]	n. 봉투, 봉지 An envelope is the rectangular paper cover in which you send a letter to someone through the post.
lie^{복습} [lai]	① v. 놓여 있다, 위치하다; 눕다, 누워 있다 ② v. 거짓말하다; n. 거짓말 If an object lies in a particular place, it is in a flat position in that place.
thoughtful[*] [θɔ́:tfəl]	a. 사려 깊은; (조용히) 생각에 잠긴 If you describe someone as thoughtful, you approve of them because they remember what other people want, need, or feel, and try not to upset them.
caring [kéəriŋ]	a. 남을 배려하는, 동정심 있는 If someone is caring, they are affectionate, helpful, and sympathetic.
row^{복습} [rou]	① n. 열, 줄 ② v. 노를 젓다, 배를 젓다; n. 노 젓기 A row of things or people is a number of them arranged in a line.

steal^{복습}
[stiːl]

v. 훔치다, 도둑질하다
If you steal something from someone, you take it away from them without their permission and without intending to return it.

rip^{복습}
[rip]

v. 찢다, 벗겨내다; n. 찢어진 틈, 잡아 찢음
When something rips or when you rip it, you tear it forcefully with your hands or with a tool such as a knife.

likable
[láikəbl]

a. 호감이 가는, 마음에 드는
Someone or something that is likeable is pleasant and easy to like.

lean^{복습}
[liːn]

v. 기울다, 기울이다, (몸을) 숙이다; ~에 기대다; ~을 ~에 기대 놓다
If you lean on or against someone or something, you rest against them so that they partly support your weight.

cane^{복습}
[kein]

n. 지팡이
A cane is a long thin stick with a curved or round top which you can use to support yourself when you are walking.

stoop
[stuːp]

n. 현관 입구의 계단
A stoop is a small platform at the door of a building, with steps leading up to it.

1분에 몇 단어를 읽는지 리딩 속도를 측정해보세요.

$$\frac{122 \text{ words}}{\text{reading time (} \quad \text{) sec}} \times 60 = (\quad) \text{ WPM}$$

Build Your Vocabulary

crumple^{복습}
[krʌmpl]

v. 구기다, 쭈글쭈글하게 하다; 구겨지다; n. 주름
If you crumple something such as paper or cloth, or if it crumples, it is squashed and becomes full of untidy creases and folds.

invent**
[invént]

v. (상상력으로) 만들다; 발명하다, 고안하다
If you invent a story or excuse, you try to make other people believe that it is true when in fact it is not.

hop^{복습}
[hap]

v. 깡충 뛰다, 뛰어오르다; n. 깡충깡충 뜀
If you hop, you move along by jumping.

vote^{복습}
[vout]

n. 투표, 투표권; v. 투표하다
A vote is a choice made by a particular person or group in a meeting or an election.

1분에 몇 단어를 읽는지 리딩 속도를 측정해보세요.

$$\frac{624 \text{ words}}{\text{reading time (\quad) sec}} \times 60 = (\quad) \text{ WPM}$$

Build Your Vocabulary

light^{복습}
[lait]

a. (날이) 밝은; n. 빛; (빛을) 비추다; 불을 붙이다
If it is light, the sun is providing light at the beginning or end of the day.

anxious***
[ǽŋkʃəs]

a. 열망하는, 간절히 바라는; 걱정하는, 염려하는 (anxiously ad. 열망하여)
If you are anxious to do something or anxious that something should happen, you very much want to do it or very much want it to happen.

compose*
[kəmpóuz]

v. (마음을) 가라앉히다, 가다듬다; 조립하다, 구성하다
If you compose yourself or if you compose your features, you succeed in becoming calm after you have been angry, excited, or upset.

count^{복습}
[kaunt]

v. 수를 세다, 계산하다; 중요하다; (정식으로) 인정되다; n. 셈, 계산
When you count, you say all the numbers one after another up to a particular number.

pause**
[pɔːz]

v. 중단하다, 잠시 멈추다; n. 멈춤, 중지
If you pause while you are doing something, you stop for a short period and then continue.

faint^{복습}
[feint]

v. 기절하다; a. 희미한, 어렴풋한
If you faint, you lose consciousness for a short time, especially because you are hungry, or because of pain, heat, or shock.

innocent^{복습}
[ínəsənt]

a. 순진한; 잘못이 없는, 결백한 (innocently ad. 순진하게)
If someone is innocent, they have no experience or knowledge of the more complex or unpleasant aspects of life.

allow^{복습}
[əláu]

v. 허락하다, ~하게 두다; 인정하다
If someone is allowed to do something, it is all right for them to do it and they will not get into trouble.

exact^{복습}
[igzǽkt]

a. 정확한, 정밀한 (exactly ad. 정확하게, 꼭)
Exact means correct in every detail.

alike^{복습}
[əláik]

a. (아주) 비슷한
If two or more things are alike, they are similar in some way.

sock^{복습}
[sak]

n. 양말
Socks are pieces of clothing which cover your foot and ankle and are worn inside shoes.

flowery
[fláuəri]

a. 꽃무늬의, 꽃무늬로 장식된
Flowery cloth, paper, or china has a lot of flowers printed or painted on it.

154

horror^{복습}
[hɔ́:rər]

n. 공포, 전율
Horror is a feeling of great shock, fear, and worry caused by something extremely unpleasant.

wrap^{복습}
[ræp]

v. 포장하다; 감싸다; n. 싸개, 덮개
When you wrap something, you fold paper or cloth tightly round it to cover it completely, for example in order to protect it or so that you can give it to someone as a present.

doorway^{복습}
[dɔ́:rwèi]

n. 출입구
A doorway is a space in a wall where a door opens and closes.

pillow^{복습}
[pílou]

n. 베개
A pillow is a rectangular cushion which you rest your head on when you are in bed.

greet^{복습}
[gri:t]

v. 인사하다; 환영하다, 맞이하다
When you greet someone, you say 'Hello' or shake hands with them.

big deal^{복습}
[bíg di:l]

n. 대단한 것, 큰 일; **intl.** 그게 무슨 대수라고! (no big deal **idiom** 별일 아니다)
If you san something is no big deal, you mean that it is not important or not a problem.

race^{복습}
[reis]

① n. 경주; v. 질주하다, 달리다; 경주하다 ② n. 인종, 민족
A race is a competition to see who is the fastest, for example in running, swimming, or driving.

occur^{**}
[əkɔ́:r]

v. 일어나다, 생기다; 생각이 떠오르다
When something occurs, it happens.

creep[*]
[kri:p]

v. (crept–crept) 살금살금 움직이다, 기다; n. 포복
If something creeps somewhere, it moves very slowly.

1분에 몇 단어를 읽는지 리딩 속도를 측정해보세요

$$\frac{592\ words}{reading\ time\ (\qquad)\ sec} \times 60 = (\qquad)\ WPM$$

Build Your Vocabulary

cone[*]
[koun]

n. 원뿔, 원뿔 모양의 물건
A cone is a shape with a circular base and smooth curved sides ending in a point at the top.

fling[**]
[fliŋ]

v. (flung–flung) (거칠게) 내던지다, 던지다, 내밀다
If you fling something somewhere, you throw it there using a lot of force.

bow[*]
[bou]

① n. 나비 모양 매듭; 활 ② v. 머리를 숙이다, 굽히다
A bow is a knot with two loops and two loose ends that is used in tying shoelaces and ribbons.

utter[복습]
[ʌ́tər]

v. (신음 소리 · 한숨 등을) 내다, 지르다; 말하다, 발언하다
If someone utters sounds or words, they say them.

desperate[복습]
[déspərət]

a. 필사적인; 자포자기의; 절망적인 (desperately ad. 필사적으로)
If you are desperate for something or desperate to do something, you want or need it very much indeed.

hardly[복습]
[háːrdli]

ad. 거의 ~아니다, 전혀 ~않다
When you say you can hardly do something, you are emphasizing that it is very difficult for you to do it.

tear[복습]
[tiər]

① v. (tore–torn) 찢다, 찢어지다; n. 찢음 ② n. 눈물
If you tear paper, cloth, or another material, or if it tears, you pull it into two pieces or you pull it so that a hole appears in it.

drawer[복습]
[drɔːr]

n. 서랍
A drawer is part of a desk, chest, or other piece of furniture that is shaped like a box and is designed for putting things in.

sink[복습]
[siŋk]

n. (부엌의) 싱크대, 개수대; 세면대; v. 가라앉다, 빠지다
A sink is a large fixed container in a kitchen, with taps to supply water. It is mainly used for washing dishes.

crook
[kruk]

v. 구부리다, 구부러지다; n. 갈고리
If you crook your arm or finger, you bend it.

hall[복습]
[hɔːl]

n. (건물 입구 안쪽의) 현관; (건물 안의) 복도
The hall in a house or flat is the area just inside the front door, into which some of the other rooms open.

stare[복습]
[stɛər]

v. 응시하다, 뚫어지게 보다
If you stare at someone or something, you look at them for a long time.

disbelief^{복습}
[dɪsbɪliːf]

n. 믿기지 않음, 불신감
Disbelief is not believing that something is true or real.

wail^{복습}
[weil]

v. (큰소리로) 울부짖다, 통곡하다; n. 울부짖음, 비탄
If someone wails, they make long, loud, high-pitched cries which express sorrow or pain.

rip^{복습}
[rip]

v. 찢다, 벗겨내다; n. 찢어진 틈, 잡아 찢음
When something rips or when you rip it, you tear it forcefully with your hands or with a tool such as a knife.

sidewalk^{복습}
[sáidwɔːk]

n. (포장한) 보도, 인도
A sidewalk is a path with a hard surface by the side of a road.

block^{복습}
[blak]

n. (도로로 나뉘는) 구역, 블록; 사각형 덩어리; v. (지나가지 못하게) 막다, 차단하다
A block in a town is an area of land with streets on all its sides.

sigh^{복습}
[sai]

v. 한숨 쉬다; n. 한숨, 탄식
When you sigh, you let out a deep breath, as a way of expressing feelings such as disappointment, tiredness, or pleasure.

tremble^{복습}
[trembl]

v. 떨다, 떨리다
If you tremble, you shake slightly because you are frightened or cold.

shiver[*]
[ʃívər]

v. (추위 · 공포로) 후들후들 떨다; 전율하다; n. 떨림, 전율
When you shiver, your body shakes slightly because you are cold or frightened.

curb[*]
[kəːrb]

n. (= kerb) 도로 경계석, (차도 가의) 연석
The curb is the raised edge of a pavement or sidewalk which separates it from the road.

patient^{복습}
[péiʃənt]

a. 인내심 있는, 참을성 있는; n. 환자 (impatiently ad. 참을성 없게)
If you are patient, you stay calm and do not get annoyed, for example when something takes a long time, or when someone is not doing what you want them to do.

assure^{복습}
[əʃúər]

v. 단언하다, 확신하다, 보증하다 (assuringly ad. 장담하여, 보장하며)
If you assure someone that something is true or will happen, you tell them that it is definitely true or will definitely happen, often in order to make them less worried.

shrug^{복습}
[ʃrʌg]

v. (양 손바닥을 내보이면서 어깨를) 으쓱하다; n. 으쓱하기
If you shrug, you raise your shoulders to show that you are not interested in something or that you do not know or care about something.

dumb^{복습}
[dʌm]

a. 멍청한, 바보 같은; 벙어리의, 말을 하지 않는
If you say that something is dumb, you think that it is silly and annoying.

anxious^{복습}
[ǽŋkʃəs]

a. 열망하는, 간절히 바라는; 걱정하는, 염려하는 (anxiously ad. 열망하여)
If you are anxious to do something or anxious that something should happen, you very much want to do it or very much want it to happen.

1. Why did Colleen's mother think that Bradley was hungry?
   A. Bradley's stomach growled.
   B. Bradley sat down at the picnic table.
   C. Bradley asked for a slice of cake.
   D. Bradley went to Colleen's refrigerator.

2. How did Chicken, the dog, act toward Bradley when compared to other people?
   A. He liked Bradley but was usually afraid of others.
   B. He liked Bradley but was usually mean toward others.
   C. He hated Bradley but was usually nice toward others.
   D. He was afraid of Bradley but was usually nice toward others.

3. Why did the losers of the race receive one point instead of nothing?
   A. It was because they could all win prizes with points.
   B. It was because it was easier to keep track of points.
   C. It was because they could trade their points with others.
   D. It was because the losers didn't feel as bad.

4. Why was Colleen never on Bradley's team?

   A. Because she hated Bradley.

   B. Because she was afraid that Bradley might beat her up.

   C. Because Jeff and Bradley were never on the same team, and Colleen was always with Jeff.

   D. Because Jeff and Bradley were always on the same team, and Colleen was never with Jeff.

5. Who was most disappointed about the three-legged race teams and why?

   A. Jeff, because he wanted to be paired with Colleen.

   B. Jeff, because he wanted to be paired with Colleen.

   C. Bradley, because he wanted to be paired with Melinda.

   D. Karen, because it would have been exciting with Bradley.

6. Who came in first place for points and what did he choose as a prize?

   A. Jeff came in first and chose a harmonica.

   B. Jeff came in first and chose a doll's dress.

   C. Bradley came in first and chose a harmonica.

   D. Bradley came in first and chose a doll's dress.

7. What did Bradley mail to Carla at her new school?

   A. He mailed her a letter and his arithmetic test.

   B. He mailed her a letter and Ronnie.

   C. He mailed her a letter and Bartholomew.

   D. He mailed her a letter and a replica of the human heart.

1분에 몇 단어를 읽는지 리딩 속도를 측정해보세요.

$$\frac{1{,}372 \text{ words}}{\text{reading time ( ) sec}} \times 60 = (\quad) \text{ WPM}$$

Build Your Vocabulary

poke*
[pouk]

v. 찌르다, 쑤시다; n. 찌름, 쑤심
If you poke someone or something, you quickly push them with your finger or with a sharp object.

elbow^{복습}
[élbou]

v. 팔꿈치로 쿡 찌르다; n. 팔꿈치
If you elbow people aside or elbow your way somewhere, you push people with your elbows in order to move somewhere.

whisper^{복습}
[hwíspər]

v. 속삭이다
When you whisper, you say something very quietly.

nod^{복습}
[nad]

v. 끄덕이다, 끄덕여 표시하다; n. (동의 · 인사 · 신호 · 명령의) 끄덕임
If you nod, you move your head downward and upward to show agreement, understanding, or approval.

backyard*
[bǽkjá:rd]

n. (주택에 딸린 잔디밭이 있는) 뒤뜰
A backyard is an area of land at the back of a house.

plate^{복습}
[pleit]

n. 접시, 그릇 (paper plate n. 1회용 종이 접시)
A plate is a round or oval flat dish that is used to hold food.

puzzle^{복습}
[pʌzl]

v. 곤혹스럽게 하다, 난처하게 하다; n. 수수께끼, 어려운 문제
If something puzzles you, you do not understand it and feel confused.

bump^{복습}
[bʌmp]

v. (쿵 하고) 부딪치다, 충돌하다; n. 충돌; 혹
If you bump into something or someone, you accidentally hit them while you are moving.

bend^{복습}
[bend]

v. (bent–bent) 구부리다, 굽히다, 숙이다; n. 커브, 굽음
When you bend, you move the top part of your body downward and forward.

knock^{복습}
[nak]

v. 치다, 부수다; (문을) 두드리다, 노크하다; n. 노크; 타격
If you knock something, you touch or hit it roughly, especially so that it falls or moves.

hysterical^{복습}
[histérikəl]

a. 히스테리 상태의, 발작적인
Someone who is hysterical is in a state of uncontrolled excitement, anger, or panic.

helpless^{복습}
[hélplis]

a. 무력한, 속수무책의 (helplessly ad. 무력하게, 어쩔 수 없이)
If you are helpless, you do not have the strength or power to do anything useful or to control or protect yourself.

pale**
[peil]

a. 창백한; 옅은, 연한; 희미한; v. 옅어지다
If someone looks pale, their face looks a lighter color than usual, usually because they are ill, frightened, or shocked.

dash^{복습}
[dæʃ]

v. 돌진하다; 내던지다; n. 돌격
If you dash somewhere, you run or go there quickly and suddenly.

muddy*
[mʌ́di]

a. 진흙투성이의; 흐린, 탁한
Something that is muddy contains mud or is covered in mud.

paw*
[pɔː]

n. (동물·갈고리 발톱이 있는) 발; v. 앞발로 차다
The paws of an animal such as a cat, dog, or bear are its feet, which have claws for gripping things and soft pads for walking on.

scold^{복습}
[skould]

v. 꾸짖다, 잔소리하다
If you scold someone, you speak angrily to them because they have done something wrong.

wiry
[wáiəri]

a. 억센, 빳빳한; 철사로 만든
Something such as hair or grass that is wiry is stiff and rough to touch.

pat^{복습}
[pæt]

v. 톡톡 가볍게 치다, 쓰다듬다; n. 쓰다듬기
If you pat something or someone, you tap them lightly, usually with your hand held flat.

split**
[split]

v. (split–split) 쪼개다, 찢다, 째다; n. 분열
If something splits or if you split it, it is divided into two or more parts.

race^{복습}
[reis]

① n. 경주; v. 질주하다, 달리다; 경주하다 (relay race n. 계주) ② n. 인종, 민족
A race is a competition to see who is the fastest, for example in running, swimming, or driving.

separate^{복습}
[sépərèit]

a. 개개의, 개별적인; v. 가르다, 떼다, 분리하다
If you refer to separate things, you mean several different things, rather than just one thing.

slap^{복습}
[slæp]

v. 찰싹 때리다; 털썩 놓다; n. 찰싹 (때림)
If you slap someone, you hit them with the palm of your hand.

yell^{복습}
[jel]

v. 소리치다, 고함치다; n. 고함소리, 부르짖음
If you yell, you shout loudly, usually because you are excited, angry, or in pain.

stick^{복습}
[stik]

① v. 내밀다; 찔러 넣다, 찌르다; 붙이다, 달라붙다 ② n. 막대기, 지팡이
If something is sticking out from a surface or object, it extends up or away from it.

holler^{복습}
[hálər]

v. 고함지르다, 큰 소리로 부르다; n. 외침, 큰 소리
If you holler, you shout loudly.

spin^{복습}
[spin]

v. (spun–spun) 돌다, 맴돌리다; 오래[질질] 끌다; n. 회전
If something spins or if you spin it, it turns quickly around a central point.

in time^{복습}

idiom 제시간에, 늦지 않고, 때맞추어
If you do something in time, it means that you are not late to do it.

bark*
[ba:rk]

v. 짖다; 고함치다, 소리 지르며 말하다
When a dog barks, it makes a short, loud noise, once or several times.

beat복습
[bi:t]

v. 패배시키다, 이기다; 치다, 두드리다; (심장이) 고동치다; n. [음악] 박자, 고동
If you beat someone in a competition or election, you defeat them.

slip복습
[slip]

v. 미끄러지다; 살짝 나오다, 살짝 들어가다
If you slip, you accidentally slide and lose your balance.

charge복습
[ʧa:rdʒ]

v. 돌격하다, 돌진하다; 청구하다; n. 요금; 책임
If you charge toward someone or something, you move quickly and aggressively toward them.

cheer복습
[ʧiər]

v. 환호성을 지르다, 응원하다; n. 환호(성)
When people cheer, they shout loudly to show their approval or to encourage someone who is doing something such as taking part in a game.

catch one's breath

idiom 한숨 돌리다, 잠시 숨을 가다듬다; 숨을 죽이다
When you catch your breath while you are doing something energetic, you stop for a short time so that you can start breathing normally again.

interrupt복습
[intərʌpt]

v. 방해하다, 가로막다, 저지하다
If you interrupt someone who is speaking, you say or do something that causes them to stop.

trade복습
[treid]

v. 교환하다; 장사하다; n. 교환; 무역
If someone trades one thing for another or if two people trade things, they agree to exchange one thing for the other thing.

count복습
[kaunt]

v. 수를 세다, 계산하다; 중요하다; (정식으로) 인정되다; n. 셈, 계산
If you count all the things in a group, you add them up in order to find how many there are.

keep track of

idiom ~을 놓치지 않다; ~의 진로를 쫓다
If you keep track of something, you remember about the number of something or the time.

delight복습
[diláit]

n. 기쁨, 즐거움; v. 즐겁게 하다, 매우 기쁘게 하다
Delight is a feeling of very great pleasure.

switch*
[swiʧ]

v. 바꾸다, 교환하다; n. 전환, 변경; 스위치
If you switch two things, you replace one with the other.

hop복습
[hap]

v. 깡충 뛰다, 뛰어오르다; n. 깡충깡충 뜀 (hopper n. 깡충깡충 뛰는 사람)
If you hop, you move along by jumping.

root
[ru:t]

v. 응원하다; 뿌리박게 하다; 정착하다; n. 뿌리
If you root for someone, you support or encourage them in a sports competition or when they are in a difficult situation.

beam복습
[bi:m]

v. 활짝 웃다; 비추다; n. 환한 얼굴; 빛줄기; [건축] 들보, 기둥
If you say that someone is beaming, you mean that they have a big smile on their face because they are happy, pleased, or proud about something.

allow ^{복습}
[əláu]

v. 허락하다, ~하게 두다; 인정하다
If someone is allowed to do something, it is all right for them to do it and they will not get into trouble.

scare ^{복습}
[skɛər]

v. 위협하다, 겁나게 하다 (scared a. 무서워하는, 겁먹은)
If something scares you, it frightens or worries you.

announce ^{복습}
[ənáuns]

v. 발표하다, 알리다
If you announce a piece of news or an intention, especially something that people may not like, you say it loudly and clearly, so that everyone you are with can hear it.

somersault
[sʌ́mərsɔ̀:lt]

n. 재주넘기, 공중제비; v. 재주넘기를 하다
If someone or something does a somersault, they turn over completely in the air.

anxious ^{복습}
[ǽŋkʃəs]

a. 걱정하는, 염려하는; 열망하는, 간절히 바라는 (anxiously ad. 걱정스럽게)
If you are anxious, you are nervous or worried about something.

hilarious
[hiléəriəs]

a. 아주 우스운, 재미있는
If something is hilarious, it is extremely funny and makes you laugh a lot.

flop ^{복습}
[flap]

v. 펄썩[털썩] 쓰러지다; 퍼덕거리다; n. 펄썩 떨어짐
If something flops onto something else, it falls there heavily or untidily.

lick ^{복습}
[lik]

v. 핥다; n. 한 번 핥기, 핥아먹기
When people or animals lick something, they move their tongue across its surface.

blush ^{복습}
[blʌʃ]

v. 얼굴을 붉히다, (얼굴이) 빨개지다; n. 얼굴을 붉힘, 홍조
When you blush, your face becomes redder than usual because you are ashamed or embarrassed.

Check Your Reading Speed

1분에 몇 단어를 읽는지 리딩 속도를 측정해보세요.

$$\frac{1{,}447 \text{ words}}{\text{reading time (}\quad\text{) sec}} \times 60 = (\quad) \text{ WPM}$$

Build Your Vocabulary

race^{복습}
[reis]

① n. 경주; v. 질주하다, 달리다; 경주하다 ② n. 인종, 민족
A race is a competition to see who is the fastest, for example in running, swimming, or driving.

pair**
[pɛər]

v. 둘씩 짝이 되다, 짝을 짓다; n. 한 쌍; (쌍을 이룬 것의) 한 쪽
If you pair up with someone, you form a pair or pairs with them in order to work or play a game.

side by side^{복습}

idiom 나란히
If two people or things are side by side, they are next to each other.

tie^{복습}
[tai]

v. 매다, 끈을 묶다; n. 넥타이
If you tie a piece of string or cloth around something or tie something with a piece of string or cloth, you put the piece of string or cloth around it and fasten the ends together.

proper**
[prápər]

a. 적합한, 알맞은
If you say that a way of behaving is proper, you mean that it is considered socially acceptable and right.

fence**
[fens]

n. 울타리, 담; v. 둘러막다
A fence is a barrier between two areas of land, made of wood or wire supported by posts.

caution**
[kɔ́ːʃən]

v. 경고하다, 주의시키다; n. 경고, 주의; 조심, 신중
If someone cautions you, they warn you about problems or danger.

nod^{복습}
[nad]

v. 끄덕이다, 끄덕여 표시하다; n. (동의 · 인사 · 신호 · 명령의) 끄덕임
If you nod, you move your head downward and upward to show agreement, understanding, or approval.

tumble*
[tʌmbl]

v. 굴러 떨어지다, 넘어지다; n. 추락; 폭락
If someone or something tumbles somewhere, they fall there with a rolling or bouncing movement.

unison
[júːnisn]

n. 조화, 화합, 일치 (in unison idiom 일치하여, 일제히)
If people do something in unison, they do the same thing at the same time.

smash^{복습}
[smæʃ]

v. 세게 충돌하다; 때려 부수다, 깨뜨리다; n. 강타; 부서지는 소리; 분쇄
If you smash into someone or something, you hit them or it very hard, causing damage.

164

charge ^{복습}
[ʧɑːrdʒ]

v. 돌격하다, 돌진하다; 청구하다; n. 요금; 책임
If you charge toward someone or something, you move quickly and aggressively toward them.

stumble ^{복습}
[stʌmbl]

v. 비틀거리며 걷다, 발부리가 걸리다; n. 비틀거림
If you stumble, you put your foot down awkwardly while you are walking or running and nearly fall over.

pile ^{복습}
[pail]

n. 쌓아 올린 더미; 다수; v. 쌓아 올리다; 쌓이다
A pile of things is a mass of them that is high in the middle and has sloping sides.

beat ^{복습}
[biːt]

n. [음악] 박자, 고동; v. 패배시키다, 이기다; 치다, 두드리다; (심장이) 고동치다
The beat of a piece of music is the main rhythm that it has.

dive ^{복습}
[daiv]

v. 뛰어들다, 급히 움직이다
If you dive in a particular direction or into a particular place, you jump or move there quickly.

crawl ^{복습}
[krɔːl]

v. 기어가다, 느릿느릿 가다; n. 기어감; 서행
When you crawl, you move forward on your hands and knees.

tangle *
[tæŋgl]

v. 엉키다, 얽히게 하다; n. 엉킴; 혼란
If something is tangled or tangles, it becomes twisted together in an untidy way.

gather ^{복습}
[gǽðər]

v. 모이다, 집합하다; 모으다, 끌다
If people gather somewhere or if someone gathers people somewhere, they come together in a group.

particular **
[pərtíkjələr]

a. 특정한, 특별한, 특유의 (in particular idiom 특별히)
You use particular to emphasize that you are talking about one thing or one kind of thing rather than other similar ones.

hush *
[hʌʃ]

v. 침묵하다; int. 쉿, 조용히 해; n. 침묵, 고요함
If you hush someone or if they hush, they stop speaking or making a noise.

announce ^{복습}
[ənáuns]

v. 발표하다, 알리다
If you announce a piece of news or an intention, especially something that people may not like, you say it loudly and clearly, so that everyone you are with can hear it.

pause ^{복습}
[pɔːz]

v. 중단하다, 잠시 멈추다; n. 멈춤, 중지
If you pause while you are doing something, you stop for a short period and then continue.

suspenseful
[səspénsfəl]

a. 긴장감 넘치는 (suspensefully ad. 긴장감이 넘치게)
A suspenseful story makes you feel excited or anxious about what is going to happen in the story next.

somersault ^{복습}
[sʌ́mərsɔ̀ːlt]

n. 재주넘기, 공중제비; v. 재주넘기를 하다
If someone or something does a somersault, they turn over completely in the air.

clap ^{복습}
[klæp]

v. 박수를 치다; n. 박수
When you clap, you hit your hands together to show appreciation or attract attention.

makeup* [méikʌp]
n. 화장품; 화장, 메이크업; 조립, 구조
Makeup consists of things such as lipstick, eye shadow, and powder which some women put on their faces to make themselves look more attractive or which actors use to change or improve their appearance.

perfume* [pə́:rfju:m]
n. 향수; 향기, 방향
Perfume is a pleasant-smelling liquid which women put on their skin to make themselves smell nice.

ornament* [ɔ́:rnəmənt]
n. 장신구, 장식품; 꾸밈; v. 꾸미다, 장식하다
An ornament is an attractive object that you display in your home or in your garden.

candle* [kǽndl]
n. 양초, 등불
A candle is a stick of hard wax with a piece of string called a wick through the middle. You light the wick in order to give a steady flame that provides light.

mess^{복습} [mes]
n. 엉망진창, 난잡함; v. 망쳐놓다, 방해하다
If you say that something is a mess or in a mess, you think that it is in an untidy state.

urge^{복습} [ə:rdʒ]
v. 촉구하다, 충고하다, 재촉하다; n. (강한) 충동
If you urge someone to do something, you try hard to persuade them to do it.

neat^{복습} [ni:t]
a. 멋진, 훌륭한; 말끔한, 깔끔한
If you say that something is neat, you mean that it is very good.

swing^{복습} [swiŋ]
v. 휘두르다; (한 점을 축으로 하여) 빙 돌다, 휙 움직이다
If something swings in a particular direction or if you swing it in that direction, it moves in that direction with a smooth, curving movement.

smack* [smæk]
v. 강타하다, 때리다, 찰싹 치다; n. 찰싹 때리기
If you smack something somewhere, you put it or throw it there so that it makes a loud, sharp noise.

exclaim^{복습} [ikskléim]
v. 외치다, 소리치다
If you exclaim, you say or shout something suddenly because of surprise, fear and pleasure.

sink^{복습} [siŋk]
v. (sank–sunk) 가라앉다, 빠지다; n. (부엌의) 싱크대, 개수대; 세면대
(one's heart sinks idiom 가슴이 철렁하다)
If your heart sink, you become depressed or lose hope.

terrible^{복습} [térəbl]
a. 심한, 지독한; 무서운, 소름끼치는
A terrible experience or situation is very serious or very unpleasant.

tease^{복습} [ti:z]
v. 놀리다, 장난하다; n. 장난, 놀림
To tease someone means to laugh at them or make jokes about them in order to embarrass, annoy, or upset them.

big deal^{복습} [bíg di:l]
intl. 그게 무슨 대수라고!; n. 대단한 것, 큰 일
You can say 'big deal' to someone to show that you are not impressed by something that they consider important or impressive.

immature
[iməʃûər]

a. 미숙한, 유치한; 미완성의
If you describe someone as immature, you are being critical of them because they do not behave in a sensible or responsible way.

wrap^{복습}
[ræp]

v. 포장하다; 감싸다; n. 싸개, 덮개
When you wrap something, you fold paper or cloth tightly round it to cover it completely, for example in order to protect it or so that you can give it to someone as a present.

replica
[réplikə]

n. 복제품, 모사품
A replica of something such as a statue, building, or weapon is an accurate copy of it.

blood vessel
[blʌd vèsəl]

n. 혈관
Blood vessels are the narrow tubes through which your blood flows.

take apart

idiom 해체하다, 분해하다
If you take something apart, you separate it into the pieces that it is made of.

all along

idiom 처음부터, 내내, 계속
If something have been there all along, it is there from the very beginning.

light^{복습}
[lait]

a. (날이) 밝은; n. 빛; (빛을) 비추다; 불을 붙이다
If it is light, the sun is providing light at the beginning or end of the day.

dangle
[dǽŋgl]

v. 매달다, 매달리다; n. 매달린 것
If something dangles from somewhere or if you dangle it somewhere, it hangs or swings loosely.

1분에 몇 단어를 읽는지 리딩 속도를 측정해보세요.

$$\frac{216 \text{ words}}{\text{reading time } (\quad) \text{ sec}} \times 60 = (\quad) \text{ WPM}$$

Build Your Vocabulary

yell^{복습}
[jel]

v. 소리치다, 고함치다; n. 고함소리, 부르짖음
If you yell, you shout loudly, usually because you are excited, angry, or in pain.

arithmetic^{복습}
[əríθmətik]

n. 산수, 셈
Arithmetic is the part of mathematics that is concerned with the addition, subtraction, multiplication, and division of numbers.

rip^{복습}
[rip]

v. 찢다, 벗겨내다; n. 찢어진 틈, 잡아 찢음
When something rips or when you rip it, you tear it forcefully with your hands or with a tool such as a knife.

kindergarten^{복습}
[kíndərgàːrtn]

n. 유치원
A kindergarten is an informal kind of school for very young children, where they learn things by playing.

bet^{복습}
[bet]

v. 틀림없이 ～이다, ～라고 확신하다; 걸다, 내기를 하다; n. 내기, 건 돈
You use expressions such as 'I bet', 'I'll bet', and 'you can bet' to indicate that you are sure something is true.

somersault^{복습}
[sʌ́mərsɔ̀ːlt]

n. 재주넘기, 공중제비; v. 재주넘기를 하다
If someone or something does a somersault, they turn over completely in the air.

fold^{복습}
[fould]

v. 접다, 접어 포개다; (손·팔·다리를) 끼다, 포개다
If you fold something such as a piece of paper or cloth, you bend it so that one part covers another part, often pressing the edge so that it stays in place.

envelope^{복습}
[énvəlòup]

n. 봉투, 봉지
An envelope is the rectangular paper cover in which you send a letter to someone through the post.

address***
[ədrés]

v. ～에게 보내다, 주소를 쓰다; ～에게 말을 걸다; 연설하다; n. 연설; 주소
If a letter, envelope, or parcel is addressed to you, your name and address have been written on it.

stare^{복습}
[stɛər]

v. 응시하다, 뚫어지게 보다
If you stare at someone or something, you look at them for a long time.

bulge^{복습}
[bʌldʒ]

n. 불룩한 것; v. 툭 튀어 나오다, 부풀어 오르다
Bulges are lumps that stick out from a surface which is otherwise flat or smooth.

frown ^{복습}
[fraun]

v. 얼굴을 찡그리다, 눈살을 찌푸리다: n. 찌푸린 얼굴

When someone frowns, their eyebrows become drawn together, because they are annoyed or puzzled.

수고하셨습니다!

드디어 끝까지 다 읽으셨군요! 축하드립니다! 여러분은 이 책을 통해 총 36,671개의 단어를 읽으셨고, 800개 이상의 어휘와 표현들을 익히셨습니다. 이 책에 나온 어휘는 다른 원서를 읽을 때에도 빈번히 만날 수 있는 필수 어휘들입니다. 이 책을 읽었던 경험은 비슷한 수준의 다른 원서들을 읽을 때 큰 도움이 될 것입니다.

이제 자신의 상황에 맞게 원서를 반복해서 읽거나, 오디오북을 들어 볼 수 있습니다. 혹은 비슷한 수준의 다른 원서를 찾아 읽는 것도 좋습니다. 일단 원서를 완독한 뒤에 어떻게 계속 영어 공부를 이어갈 수 있을지, 도움말을 꼼꼼히 살펴보고 각자 상황에 맞게 적용해 보세요!

리딩(Reading)을 확실하게 다지고 싶다면? 반복해서 읽어 보세요!

리딩 실력을 탄탄하게 다지고 싶다면, 같은 원서를 2~3번 반복해서 읽을 것을 권합니다. 같은 책을 여러 번 읽으면 지루할 것 같지만, 꼭 그렇지도 않습니다. 반복해서 읽을 때 처음과 주안점을 다르게 두면, 전혀 다른 느낌으로 재미있게 읽을 수 있습니다.

처음 원서를 읽을 때는 생소한 단어들과 스토리로 인해 읽으면서 곧바로 이해하기가 매우 힘들 수 있습니다. 전체 맥락을 잡고 읽어도 약간 버거운 느낌이지요. 하지만 반복해서 읽기 시작하면 달라집니다. 일단 내용을 파악한 상황이기 때문에 문장 구조나 어휘의 활용에 더 집중하게 되고, 조금 더 깊이 있게 읽을 수 있습니다. 좋은 표현과 문장을 수집하고 메모할 만한 여유도 생기게 되지요. 어휘도 많이 익숙해졌기 때문에 리딩 속도에도 탄력이 붙습니다. 처음 읽을 때는 '내용'에서 재미를 느꼈다면, 반복해서 읽을 때에는 '영어'에서 재미를 느끼게 되는 것입니다. 따라서 리딩 실력을 더욱 확고하게 다지고자 한다면, 같은 책을 2~3회 정도 반복해서 읽을 것을 권해 드립니다.

리스닝(Listening) 실력을 늘리고 싶다면?
귀를 통해서 읽어 보세요!

많은 영어 학습자들이 '리스닝이 안 돼서 문제'라고 한탄합니다. 그리고 리스닝 실력을 늘리는 방법으로 무슨 뜻인지 몰라도 반복해서 듣는 '무작정 듣기'를 선택합니다. 하지만 뜻도 모르면서 무작정 듣는 일에는 엄청난 인내력이 필요합니다. 그래서 대부분 며칠 시도하다가 포기해 버리고 말지요.

따라서 모르는 내용을 무작정 듣는 것보다는 어느 정도 알고 있는 내용을 반복해서 듣는 것이 더 효과적인 듣기 방법입니다. 그리고 이런 방식의 듣기에 활용할 수 있는 가장 좋은 교재가 오디오북입니다.

리스닝 실력을 향상하고 싶다면, 이 책에서 제공하는 오디오북을 이용해서 듣는 연습을 해 보세요. 활용법은 간단합니다. 일단 책을 한 번 완독했다면, 오디오북을 통해 다시 들어 보는 것입니다. 휴대 기기에 넣어 시간이 날 때 틈틈이 듣는 것도 좋고, 책상에 앉아 눈으로는 텍스트를 보며 귀로 읽는 것도 좋습니다. 이미 읽었던 내용이라 이해하기가 훨씬 수월하고, 애매했던 발음들도 자연스럽게 교정할 수 있습니다. 또 성우의 목소리 연기를 듣다 보면 내용이 더욱 생동감 있게 다가와 이해도가 높아지는 효과도 거둘 수 있습니다.

반대로 듣기에 자신 있는 사람이라면, 책을 읽기 전에 처음부터 오디오북을 먼저 듣는 것도 좋은 방법입니다. 귀를 통해 책을 쭉 읽어보고, 이후에 다시 눈으로 책을 읽으면서 잘 들리지 않았던 부분들을 보충하는 것이지요.

중요한 것은 내용을 따라가면서, 내용에 푹 빠져서 반복해 들어야 한다는 것입니다. 이렇게 연습을 반복해서 눈으로 읽지 않은 책이라도 '귀를 통해' 읽을 수 있을 정도가 되면, 리스닝으로 고생하는 일은 거의 없을 것입니다.

왼쪽의 QR 코드를 스마트폰으로 인식하여 정식 오디오북을 들어 보세요!
더불어 롱테일북스 홈페이지(www.longtailbooks.co.kr)에서도
오디오북 MP3 파일을 다운로드 받을 수 있습니다.

스피킹(Speaking)이 고민이라면? 소리 내어 읽어 보세요!

스피킹 역시 많은 학습자들이 고민하는 부분입니다. 스피킹이 고민이라면, 원서를 큰 소리로 읽는 낭독 훈련(Voice Reading)을 해 보세요!

'소리 내어 읽는 것이 말하기에 정말로 도움이 될까?'라고 의아한 생각이 들 수도 있습니다. 하지만 인간의 두뇌 입장에서 봤을 때, 성대 구조를 활용해서 '발화'한다는 점에서는 소리 내어 읽기와 말하기에 큰 차이가 없다고 합니다. 소리 내어 읽는 것은 '타인의 생각'을 전달하고, 직접 말하는 것은 '자신의 생각'을 전달한다는 차이가 있을 뿐, 머릿속에서 문장을 처리하고 조음기관(혀와 성대 등)을 움직여 의미를 만든다는 점에서 같은 과정인 것이지요. 따라서 소리 내어 읽는 연습을 꾸준히 하는 것은 스피킹 연습에 큰 도움이 됩니다.

소리 내어 읽기를 하는 방법은 간단합니다. 일단 오디오북을 들으면서 성우의 목소리를 최대한 따라 하며 같이 읽어 보세요. 발음뿐 아니라 억양, 어조, 느낌까지 완벽히 따라 한다고 생각하면서 소리 내어 읽습니다. 따라 읽는 것이 조금 익숙해지면, 옆의 누군가에게 이 책을 읽어 준다는 생각으로 소리 내어 계속 읽어 나갑니다. 한 번 눈과 귀로 읽었던 책이기 때문에 보다 수월하게 진행할 수 있고, 자연스럽게 어휘와 표현을 복습하는 효과도 거두게 됩니다. 또 이렇게 소리 내어 읽은 것을 녹음해서 들어 보면 스스로에게도 좋은 피드백이 됩니다.

최근 말하기가 강조되면서 소리 내어 읽기가 크게 각광을 받고 있기는 하지만, 그렇다고 소리 내어 읽기가 무조건 좋은 것만은 아닙니다. 책을 소리 내어 읽다 보면, 무의식적으로 속으로 발음을 하는 습관을 가지게 되어 리딩 속도 자체는 오히려 크게 떨어지는 현상이 발생할 수 있습니다. 따라서 빠른 리딩 속도가 중요한 수험생이나 상위권 학습자들에게는 소리 내어 읽기가 적절하지 않은 방법입니다. 효과가 좋다는 말만 믿고 무턱대고 따라 하기보다는 자신의 필요에 맞게 우선순위를 정하고 원서를 활용하는 것이 좋습니다.

라이팅(Writing)까지 욕심이 난다면? 요약하는 연습을 해 보세요!

원서를 라이팅 연습에 직접적으로 활용하는 데에는 한계가 있지만, 적절히 활용하면 원서도 유용한 라이팅 자료가 될 수 있습니다.

특히 책을 읽고 그 내용을 요약하는 연습은 큰 도움이 됩니다. 요약 훈련의 방식도 간단합니다. 원서를 읽고 그날 읽은 분량만큼 혹은 책을 다 읽고 전체 내용을 기반으로, 책 내용을 한번 요약하고 나의 느낌을 영어로 적어보는 것입니다.

이때 그 책에 나왔던 단어와 표현을 최대한 활용하여 요약하는 것이 중요합니다. 영어 표현력은 결국 얼마나 다양한 어휘로 많은 표현을 해 보았느냐가 좌우하게 됩니다. 이런 면에서 내가 읽은 책을, 그 책에 나온 문장과 어휘로 다시 표현해 보는 것은 매우 효율적인 방법입니다. 책에 나온 어휘와 표현을 단순히 읽고 무슨 말인지 아는 정도가 아니라, 실제로 직접 활용해서 쓸 수 있을 만큼 확실하게 익히게 되는 것이지요. 여기에 첨삭까지 받을 수 있는 방법이 있다면 금상첨화입니다.

이러한 '표현하기' 연습은 스피킹 훈련에도 그대로 적용될 수 있습니다. 책을 읽고 그 내용을 3분 안에 다른 사람에게 영어로 말하는 연습을 해 보세요. 순발력과 표현력을 기르는 좋은 훈련이 될 것입니다.

꾸준히 원서를 읽고 싶다면? 뉴베리 수상작을 계속 읽어 보세요!

뉴베리 상이 세계 최고 권위의 아동 문학상인 만큼, 그 수상작들은 확실히 완성도를 검증받은 작품이라고 할 수 있습니다. 특히 '쉬운 어휘로 쓰인 깊이 있는 문장'으로 이루어졌다는 점이 영어 학습자들에게 큰 호응을 얻고 있습니다. 이렇게 '검증된 원서'를 꾸준히 읽는 것은 영어 실력 향상에 큰 도움이 됩니다.

아래에 수준별로 제시된 뉴베리 수상작 목록을 보며 적절한 책들을 찾아 계속 읽어 보세요. 꼭 뉴베리 수상작이 아니더라도 마음에 드는 작가의 다른 책을 읽어 보는 것 또한 아주 좋은 방법입니다.

• 영어 초보자도 쉽게 읽을 만한 아주 쉬운 수준. 소리 내어 읽기에도 아주 적합.
Sarah, Plain and Tall★(Medal, 8,331단어), The Hundred Penny Box (Honor, 5,878단어), The Hundred Dresses★(Honor, 7,329단어), My Father's Dragon (Honor, 7,682단어), 26 Fairmount Avenue (Honor, 6,737단어)

- 중·고등학생 정도 영어 학습자라면 쉽게 읽을 수 있는 수준. 소리 내어 읽기에도 비교적 적합한 편.

Because of Winn-Dixie★(Honor, 22,123단어), What Jamie Saw (Honor, 17,203단어), Charlotte's Web (Honor, 31,938단어), Dear Mr. Henshaw (Medal, 18,145단어), Missing May (Medal, 17,509단어)

- 대학생 정도 영어 학습자라면 무난한 수준. 소리 내어 읽기에 적합하지 않음.

Number The Stars★(Medal, 27,197단어), A Single Shard (Medal, 33,726단어), The Tale of Despereaux★(Medal, 32,375단어), Hatchet★(Medal, 42,328단어), Bridge to Terabithia (Medal, 32,888단어), A Fine White Dust (Honor, 19,022단어), Jennifer, Hecate, Macbeth, William McKinley and Me, Elizabeth (Honor, 23,266단어)

- 원서 완독 경험을 가진 학습자에게 적절한 수준. 소리 내어 읽기에 적합하지 않음.

The Giver★(Medal, 43,617단어), From the Mixed-Up Files of Mrs. Basil E. Frankweiler (Medal, 30,906단어), The View from Saturday (Medal, 42,685단어), Holes★(Medal, 47,079단어), Criss Cross (Medal, 48,221단어), Walk Two Moons (Medal, 59,400단어), The Graveyard Book (Medal, 67,380단어)

뉴베리 수상작과 뉴베리 수상 작가의 좋은 작품을 엄선한 「뉴베리 컬렉션」에도 위 목록에 있는 도서 중 상당수가 포함될 예정입니다.

★ 「뉴베리 컬렉션」으로 이미 출간된 도서

어떤 책들이 출간되었는지 확인하려면, 지금 인터넷서점에서
뉴베리 컬렉션을 검색해 보세요.

뉴베리 수상작을 동영상 강의로 만나 보세요!

영어원서 전문 동영상 강의 사이트 영서당(yseodang.com)에서는 뉴베리 컬렉션 『Holes』, 『Because of Winn-Dixie』, 『The Miraculous Journey of Edward Tulane』, 『Wayside School』 시리즈 등의 동영상 강의를 제공하고 있습니다. 뉴베리 수상작 이라는 최고의 영어 교재와 EBS 출신 인기 강사가 만난 명강의! 지금 사이트를 방문해서 무료 샘플 강의를 들어 보세요!

'스피드 리딩 카페'를 통해 원서 읽기 습관을 길러 보세요!

일상에서 영어를 한마디도 쓰지 않는 비영어권 국가에서 살고 있는 우리가 영어 환경에 가장 쉽고, 편하고, 부담 없이 노출되는 방법은 바로 '영어원서 읽기'입니다. 언제 어디서든 원서를 붙잡고 읽기만 하면 곧바로 영어를 접하는 환경이 만들어지기 때문이지요. 하루에 20분씩만 꾸준히 읽는다면, 1년에 무려 120시간 동안 영어에 노출될 수 있습니다. 이러한 이유 때문에 영어 교육 전문가들이 영어 원서 읽기를 추천하는 것이지요.

하지만 원서 읽기가 좋다는 것을 알아도 막상 꾸준히 읽는 것은 쉽지 않습니다. 그럴 때에는 13만 명 이상의 회원을 보유한 국내 최대 원서 읽기 동호회 〈스피드 리딩 카페〉(cafe.naver.com/readingtc)를 방문해 보세요.

원서별로 정리된 무료 PDF 단어장과 수준별 추천 원서 목록 등 유용한 자료는 물론, 뉴베리 수상작을 포함한 다양한 원서의 리뷰를 무료로 확인할 수 있습니다. 특히 함께 모여서 원서를 읽는 '북클럽'은 중간에 포기하지 않고 원서를 끝까지 읽는 습관을 기르는 데 큰 도움이 될 것입니다.

chapters 1 to 4

1. B   Bradley Chalkers sat at his desk in the back of the room—last seat, last row. No one sat at the desk next to him or at the one in front of him. He was an island.

2. C   Bradley thought a moment, then said, "Give me a dollar or I'll spit on you."

3. D   "I'll give you a dollar if you'll be my friend," said Bradley. He held out the dollar Jeff had given him earlier.

4. A   "Hi, everybody," he answered, this time speaking for himself. He was talking to his collection of little animals.

5. A   "Mrs. Ebbel just called," said his mother. His heart fluttered. "Why didn't you tell me that tomorrow was Parents' Conference Day?" asked his mother.

6. D   Bradley's father worked in the police department. He had been shot in the leg four years ago while chasing a robber. Now he needed a cane to walk, so he worked behind a desk.

7. B   "I can't wait to meet him," the counselor interrupted. "He sounds charming, just delightful."

chapters 5 to 8

1. B   At dinner Bradley's father asked how the meeting with Bradley's teacher went. Bradley looked down at his mashed potatoes. "Fine," said his mother. "Bradley is doing very well."

2. D   Bradley looked at Jeff as if he were from outer space. "I don't need any help," he said. "I'm the smartest kid in class. Ask anyone."

3. C   He was on his way to see the new counselor. She was supposed to help him "adjust to his new environment." Now he not only didn't know how to get to her office, he had no idea how to get back to Mrs. Ebbel's class either.

4. B   He walked to the end of the hall, turned right, counted to the second door on his left, and pushed it open. A girl with red hair and a freckled face was washing her hands at the sink. When she saw Jeff, her mouth dropped open. "What are you doing in here?" she asked. "Huh?" Jeff uttered. "Get out of here!" she yelled. "This is the girls' bathroom!" Jeff froze. He covered his face with his hands, then dashed out the door.

5. A   A girl with red hair and a freckled face was washing her hands at the sink. When she saw Jeff, her mouth dropped open. "What are you doing in here?" she asked.

6. D   "I hope so. I think he needs help even more than me. You won't tell him anything I said, will you?" "No, that's one of my most important rules. I never repeat anything anyone tells me here, around the round table." "Never?" She shook her head. "What about to other teachers?" She shook it again. "What about to the principal?" "Nope."

7. C   Melinda and Lori backed away. "We only wanted to know his name," said Melinda. "And what he was doing in the girls' bathroom!" screeched Lori.

chapters 9 to 12

1. C   "Where are you going?" "Library," he said. "To get a book." "Okay, but make sure you go straight to the library. No detours, Bradley."

2. B   "Oh, I don't believe in accidents," said Carla. "You don't believe in accidents?" That was the craziest thing he'd ever heard.

3. D   When he got to Mrs. Ebbel's class, he crumpled his picture into a ball and dropped it in the wastepaper basket next to her desk.

4. D   Actually, Bradley never had been inside a girls' bathroom. It was something he'd always wanted to do, but he'd never had the courage even to peek into one. But now that he and Jeff were friends, he hoped Jeff would take him inside one. He was dying to know what they looked like. He imagined they were carpeted in gold, with pink wallpaper and red velvet toilet seats. He thought girl toilets would look nothing like boy toilets. They'd probably be more like fountains, with colored water.

5. A   "Um, now's not a good time," said Jeff. "Why not?" Jeff thought a moment. "There won't be any girls there now," he said. "They all go home to use their own bathrooms."

6. C   Jeff shrugged. "Whenever anybody says hello to me, I always say hello back."

7. B   "Colleen Verigold," said the girl. She sat down in one of the chairs around the round table and said, "I don't know who to invite to my birthday party."

1. D   "Just because you and he are friends, that doesn't mean he can't have other friends too," said Carla. "Yes it does." "Why?" "Because," he said proudly. "So long as Jeff is friends with me, nobody else will like him!"

2. A   And after he did his homework, Mrs. Ebbel might give him a gold star. Instead of scribbling, he drew little stars, one after another until the bell rang.

3. C   "They're in Mrs. Sharp's class," said Bradley. "We can wait here until they come out, then sneak up behind them." "Who?" "Those girls. We have to beat them up so they won't say hello to you."

4. D   "It won't take long," Bradley assured him. "You just have to hit them once, and they cry and run away." "But it's raining," said Jeff. It was barely misting. "Good! We can push them in the mud and get their clothes dirty. Girls hate it when their clothes get dirty." "Girls kick," warned Bradley. "They don't know how to punch, so they try to kick you." He quickened his pace until he was just a few steps behind the girls. Jeff lagged a little behind.

5. B   He had stopped crying shortly after he ran away from Melinda, but started again when he saw his mother. "They beat me up and threw me in the mud," he sobbed.

6. B   "Don't be afraid to tell me," said his mother. "They won't hurt you anymore." Bradley thought a moment. "Jeff Fishkin!" he declared. "He was the leader of the gang."

7. A   "No, I don't think she told anybody. After you left, she asked me not to tell anyone what happened. She made Lori and Colleen promise not to tell too."

chapters 17 to 20

1. B   "Man, when I saw Chalkers' eye today," said Robbie, "I just $smiled. And then when I found out you got called to the principal's office, I thought, 'Way to go, Jeff.' " "You didn't get in trouble, did you, Jeff?" asked Dan. Jeff shook his head. "They probably gave him a medal," said Russell, laughing. The others laughed too. "You like to play basketball, Jeff?" asked Andy, the boy with the basketball.

2. D   "Hey, Jeff!" Jeff didn't look up from his work. $Jeff works hard$, Bradley realized. $That's how he gets all the gold stars.$ He had to wait until after school. "Hey, Jeff," he said as soon as the bell rang. Jeff picked up his books and started out the door.

3. C   Bradley suddenly felt very nervous. "Do you want to do our homework together?" he asked. "I can come over to your house if you want, or you can come over to

mine. We can use my book. See." He showed Jeff his book.

4. A   And he was glad Jeff wasn't his friend anymore. He realized he was better off without friends. In fact, he never was friends with Jeff! *I was just pretending to be his friend.*

5. B   "Why? I'm not. I hate him. In fact"—he looked around the room—"I gave him a black eye!" He quickly glanced at Carla to see if she knew he was lying, then looked away.

6. D   "So I don't think I need to see a counselor anymore," he said, "since I have eight friends." "Okay, Jeff, if that's how you feel," said Carla. "They might think I'm weird or something," he explained.

7. D   "No, and they won't either! You know what they said? They said it was a waste of money for the school to hire you. They said you should get married and have your own children before you start telling other parents how they should raise theirs."

chapters 21 to 24

1. C   "I punched myself in the eye," he said as he walked past her. He didn't want her thinking someone else gave it to him. "I'm the only one who can beat me up."

2. B   "The doctor says I'm supposed to talk a little, just not a lot." "All right. Shall we talk about school?" "No! The doctor says if I talk about school, I'll die!"

3. D   Claudia gave him back the list. "You wrote 'Gold stars' three times," she said, shaking her head.

4. A   "You don't know her," he replied. "She'll talk about anything I want to talk about. She listens to me. She likes me!" "No she doesn't," scoffed Claudia. "That's just her job!" She walked out of his room, laughing.

5. C   "No," said Carla. "I think everyone has 'good' inside him. Everyone can feel happiness, and sadness and loneliness. But sometimes people think someone's a monster. But that's only because they can't see the 'good' that's there inside him. And then a terrible thing happens."

6. A   "And quit saying hello to me too!" "We can say hello if we want," said Melinda. "It's a free country." "I don't want you saying it to me," said Jeff. "Hello, Jeff, hello, Jeff," said Lori. "Jello, Jeff." She laughed at her mistake. "Jello, Jeff. Hello, Jello." She laughed hysterically. She slugged him in the stomach. As he bent over she hit him in the nose. Jeff flailed his arms as he tried to defend himself, but Melinda kept punching him, in the neck, in the stomach, then in the eye. Jeff fell to the ground.

7. D   All week Bradley worked on his list of topics to discuss with Carla. *It's not homework*, he kept telling himself. *In fact, it's the opposite of homework! Because if I think of some good topics, then we won't have to talk about homework.*

chapters 25 to 28

1. D   *I'm going to be good*, thought Bradley, *and then, when everybody sees how good I am, they'll know I'm not a monster.*

2. A   Bradley was so excited, he didn't realize he was putting on two different-colored socks: a blue one and a green one.

3. B   He looked around. The floor and the bottom half of the walls were covered with green tile. There were two white sinks and a paper towel dispenser. There were three toilets in three separate stalls. Each stall had a door. It looked very much like the boys' bathroom. Girl toilets appeared to be the same as boy toilets. He was disappointed.

4. A   "No, Mrs. Wilcott won't let me. I used to, a long time ago, before I met you, I used to check out books and not return them. I used to scribble in them and rip them up. So she won't let me check any books out anymore. The whole time I was there she kept watching me, saying, 'I don't want any trouble from you, Bradley.' "

5. B   "I hate socks that match," said Carla. "See." She stuck out her legs. She was wearing white pants. She had on one white sock and one black sock.

6. C   "You've never done it before," said Ronnie. "I'm doing it for Carla. Now leave me alone so I can concentrate."

7. D   "I can't figure out how to do my homework," he complained. "Will you help me?" His mother smiled. "I'd be delighted. Let me see." . . . "You'll help me?" Bradley asked his sister. "Sure, why not? I got nothing better to do." . . . "I need help," he complained. "I'll help you," said his father. "You will?" "Let's go to my office. We can work at my desk."

chapters 29 to 32

1. A   "Do you want something, Bradley?" asked Mrs. Ebbel. He looked at his homework shaking in his hand. Then he tore it in half and dropped it in the wastepaper basket next to Mrs. Ebbel's desk.

2. C   "The main thing is that you did it. And you learned some things by doing it,

didn't you?"

3. B   "No, we never have homework over the weekend." He spoke like an expert, like he'd been doing homework for years. "But we have a book report due next week. Only . . ."

4. D   "So you don't have any complaints about Miss Davis?" his mother asked seriously, getting back to the letter. "She's okay," he said without emotion. Claudia snickered. "Well, then, I won't go to the meeting," said his mother. "C'mon, let's leave your brother alone."

5. C   Bradley paid close attention as Mrs. Ebbel taught arithmetic. He nodded his head every time she said something that he already knew.

6. B   He smiled now as he remembered it. It's because of Carla's book, he thought. The book was his lucky charm. As long as he had it with him, it seemed like nothing could go wrong.

7. A   Bradley readied himself. He raised his fists in the air, then lowered them. He had an idea. "Hello, Jeff," he said. Robbie snickered. Jeff stared at him, wide-eyed. "Hello, Bradley," he replied.

chapters 33 to 36

1. D   Jeff sat down so Bradley wouldn't pass it to him. "Just shoot," he said. The rest of his team sat down too. "Shoot it!" they said. Everybody on the other team sat down too. "Shoot the ball!"

2. B   He walked into the boys' bathroom and splashed his sweaty face with cold water. He had to hold the faucet down with one hand and splash his face with the other. Colleen Verigold walked in.

3. C   Carla turned to Colleen. "So what's the big emergency? Can you say it in front of Jeff?" "He already knows," said Colleen. She looked at Jeff. "You better not tell anybody!" "I won't," Jeff promised. "Tell anybody what?" asked Carla. "Colleen walked into the boys' bathroom," said Jeff. "I was there washing my face."

4. B   "A religion," answered Carla. She got a book from her bookcase. "Here it is." She read aloud from *Raise High the Roof Beam, Carpenters* by J.D. Salinger: "'In certain Zen monasteries, it's a cardinal rule . . . that when one monk calls out "Hi" to another monk, the latter must call back "Hi!" without thinking.'" "Jeff should be a Zen monk!" Colleen exclaimed with delight.

5. D   Before dinner, while it was still light, Bradley's father, bad leg and all, taught

Bradley how to dribble. Bradley could hardly wait to show his friends.

6. C   "Oh, you can't come anymore, Melinda," said Colleen. "Why not?" she asked, obviously very hurt. "Because they're coming, and you beat them up!" "But they started it."

7. A   He pulled out a tissue, but didn't use it. "I've never been to a birthday party," he blubbered. Then he hiccupped. "Not a real one, where other kids are there." He hiccupped again, then blew his nose. "A long time ago, when I was in the third grade I went to one, but then they made me go home because I sat on the cake."

chapters 37 to 40

1. C   Her husband had a chart that showed that if the counselor was fired, there would be enough money to put a computer in every classroom. . . . "She told my son it was good to fail!" shouted a woman standing under a poster of an octopus. "She told him grades didn't matter." . . . "She's been trying to make her change religions," said Colleen's mother. "Colleen came home from school and announced she didn't want to be Catholic anymore. She wants to be a Zen monk!"

2. A   "What if there was a boy who bit his teacher?" asked a father. "What?" Carla exclaimed.

3. B   "Bradley, I have something I have to tell you," she said. "I hope you can listen to what I have to say without feeling scared or upset." He suddenly felt very scared and upset. "Tomorrow will be my last day here at Red Hill School." "Huh?" . . . "I've been transferred. I'll be teaching kindergarten at Willow Bend School. But I want to thank you, Bradley. You've made my short time here very special. I'm so glad we got to know each other."

4. D   "No! It's not fair!" He stood up. "You tricked me!" Carla stood too. She walked around the table toward him. "I hate you!" he shouted in her face.

5. A   "We finished talking," the lion told Ronnie. "We took a vote. We don't like you anymore."

6. C   "Miss Davis gave it to me yesterday," Mrs. Ebbel told him. "She explained how she accidentally ripped it." He stared at her, amazed, then noticed his book report, taped together, lying on Mrs. Ebbel's desk. At the very top, in red ink, was the word *Excellent!*

7. B   When the final bell rang, he walked directly home. The knot inside him tightened with every step he took. *I hate her! I hate her! I hate her!*

182

1. A   In the past, she had always cut Bradley's hair herself. But this time he had asked to go to a "real" barber shop. That was earlier in the week, when they were out buying the birthday present for Colleen. "You make my head look like a chili bowl," he had complained.

2. C   "I'm supposed to see my counselor. She is waiting to see me. Call the school if you don't believe me." The car stopped in the parking lot in front of the barber shop. "We're here!" his mother said sternly. "You're getting your hair cut, now."

3. B   He opened it on the playground, next to the monkey bars. Inside was the book *My Parents Didn't Steal an Elephant*, by Uriah C. Lasso, and a letter.

4. D   Bradley tried writing a letter to Carla. His father had suggested it.

5. C   When Colleen told Dena there would be a three-legged race, the room turned very quiet. Each girl wondered if she would have to run it with a boy.

6. D   Bradley hardly heard him. "Are you supposed to wear torn pants?" he asked. "What?" He ran into the kitchen. He took a sharp knife from the drawer next to the sink and cut a hole in his pants, just above the knee.

7. A   So, while the eight girls anxiously waited, Jeff was patiently trying to teach Bradley everything he knew about birthday parties.

chapters 45 to 47

1. B   Colleen's mother came in and led everyone out to the backyard. A picnic table had been set up on the patio with paper plates and cups. Bradley chose a seat and sat down. "My, this boy must be hungry!" said Colleen's mother.

2. A   "Chicken's usually afraid of everybody," said Colleen. Bradley patted his head, glad Chicken liked him.

3. D   Betty interrupted. "It would come out the same if they just gave one point to the winners and nothing to the losers," she said, "but this way the losers don't feel as bad."

4. C   They continued changing teams for each new race. He and Jeff were never allowed on the same team, and since Colleen always made sure that she was on Jeff's team, Bradley was never with her either.

5. D   Bradley was glad that he and Jeff were finally on the same team. Colleen and Jeff were happy with the teams too. As much as they liked each other, they weren't quite

ready to put their arms around each other and tie their legs together. Karen was the only one who was disappointed. She thought it would have been exciting to have been partners with Bradley.

6. C   Everyone hushed as Mrs. Verigold prepared to announce the winner. "The winner is . . ."—she paused suspensefully—". . . Bradley!" He was shocked. He had been on the winning team every time except for the three-legged race and the somersault race, but he had been having too much fun to notice. Everyone clapped their hands as he walked to the front. Mrs. Verigold gave him a blue ribbon that said First Place on it. No one had told him about the ribbon. Then he got to pick a prize. He looked through the basket. There were lots of good things from which to choose: dolls, makeup, perfume, earrings, hair ornaments. He chose a harmonica.

7. B   Bradley folded the letter and put it in the envelope. He wrote Carla's name on the outside and addressed it to Willow Bend School. Ronnie gave Bartholomew a big hug and kiss. . . . Bradley placed the little red rabbit with the broken ear inside the envelope.